P9-AOT-915

weekends with friends

weekends with friends

Maxine Clark

photography by Noel Murphy

RYLAND
PETERS
& SMALL

LONDON NEW YORK

First published in the USA
by Ryland Peters & Small, Inc.
519 Broadway, 5th Floor
New York, NY 10012
www.rylandpeters.com

10 9 8 7 6 5 4 3 2 1

Library of Congress
Cataloging-in-Publication Data

Clark, Maxine.
  Weekends with friends : cooking and
entertaining at home / Maxine Clark ;
photography by Noel Murphy.
      p. cm.
  Includes index.
  ISBN 1-84172-948-5
1. Cookery. 2. Entertaining. I. Title.
TX714.C525 2005
641.5--dc22
                        2005003593

Printed and bound in China

Senior Designer Steve Painter
Commissioning Editor
   Elsa Petersen-Schepelern
Editor Susan Stuck
Production Patricia Harrington
Art Director Gabriella Le Grazie
Publishing Director Alison Starling

Food Stylist Maxine Clark
Assistant Food Stylists
   Lizzie Harries, Susie Plant
Prop Stylist Liz Belton
Indexer Hilary Bird

Notes

• All spoon measurements are level unless
otherwise stated.

• Eggs are large unless otherwise specified.
Uncooked or partially cooked eggs should
not be served to the very old, frail, young
children, pregnant women, or those with
compromised immune systems.

Dedication

To E.P-S, with gratitude.

Author's Acknowledgments

Thank you Elsa for the opportunity to write
this book and for all the help along the way.
Thanks to Steve for his modeling talents and
chocolate treats. Thanks to Lizzie and Susie,
without whom I could not have coped. Liz
Belton's styling was inspired and Noel's
photography relaxed and atmospheric.

contents

6 planning the weekend

8 ten golden rules of relaxed entertaining

10 party food

30 brunch and snacks

42 soups and appetizers

58 main dishes

78 vegetarian

94 vegetables and salads

108 sweet things

124 drinks

134 basics and standbys

142 menu planner

143 index

planning the weekend

Don't you just envy friends who seem like natural-born hosts, cool, calm, and collected and completely unfazed by numbers? Well, we can all be like that with a little organization and forward thinking. Half an hour's planning and list-making will save so much time and anxiety when guests arrive, and will do wonders for your confidence. So take some time out and sit down quietly with a notepad and pen and start at the beginning.

Planning Ahead

When will everyone arrive, and what will the first meal be? Will it just be a cup of tea and a cake or a drink and some nibbles? Start here and draw up a list of meals and snacks, adding in drinks as well. From this, expand the list into menus, following the Ten Golden Rules on page 8. Remember, the reason for getting together in the first place is to enjoy each other's company in relaxed surroundings, enhanced by some simple and delicious food and drink, so don't put pressure on yourself to be a top chef—this isn't the time! Above all, you should make the cooking and eating fun and part of the total experience, and don't let it become a chore. Make use of the oven when it's on and cook more than one thing at a time, or cook double quantities to keep for later, or turn into another meal.

Shopping Ahead

Try to do all the shopping at once, making a note of anything you will still have to buy later. Divide your shopping list into categories—Dry Goods; Fruit and Vegetables; Meat, Poultry, and Fish; Dairy; and Miscellaneous. This will make the shopping easier. At the checkout, pack all the refrigerator items together with anything frozen, put the fruit and vegetables together, the bottles and jars in one bag or box. This will save time and effort when unpacking at home and makes any delegating of tasks easily explained. Unpack and arrange everything in their appropriate places, and organize the refrigerator. Drinks and non-perishable vegetables tend to take up a lot of space, so pack them in portable coolers if you have the space, or keep in the garage, barn, or greenhouse if it is cold outside. Try to phone in any special orders well in advance and remember to pick them up!

Check the Basics

Go through your pantry, refrigerator, and freezer and top up the basics—tea, coffee, sugar, flour, breakfast cereals, juice, eggs, milk, bread, butter. Don't forget everyday essentials like garbage bags, rolls of paper towels, plastic wrap, dish liquid, dishwasher detergent, candles and matches, paper napkins, clean dish towels, rubber gloves, aprons, and so on. If it's summertime, clean that outdoor grill and make sure you have enough fuel.

Easy Maintenance

As the weekend progresses, don't be tempted to let leftovers build up; they will take up valuable refrigerator space and you really won't use them. Keep on top of the dishes, and if not too worse for wear, try to set the breakfast table before you go to bed. If not, first up gets the task! This saves all that chaos caused by the "grazing" habit.

Above all, if everyone helps out, the weekend will be a roaring success and the focus will be on enjoying and sharing each other's company.

ten golden rules of relaxed entertaining

Most people are too busy to entertain during the week. It's on the weekend that we have the time to enjoy ourselves. Drinks for a few friends, a dinner party, brunch, or a long lunch in the garden—you might even have guests for the weekend. Apply these Golden Rules whenever you entertain—they're equally useful for small gatherings or large parties.

1

Planning the meals in advance will work miracles (and this includes breakfast). Keep it simple.

2

NEVER attempt to cook anything new when entertaining guests. Stick to what you know and are comfortable with—and do it well. If necessary, road test them on your family.

3

Always cook with ingredients that you can actually buy—if it's not in season or has to be bought from a Thai market two hours' drive away, think again or plan the marketing well in advance.

4

Check who eats what. If there is only one vegetarian among your guests, then plan a complete meal around that—if the food is good, then no one will notice. Asian food is a good choice.

5

Do as much of the marketing as possible in good time, making lists (sounds boring, but there's less chance of forgetting something). You can get real satisfaction from crossing things off the list.

6

If you aren't confident about your own cooking, make use of all the cooking short cuts and time-savers at your disposal. There are lots of reliable products out there, such as spice pastes (more aromatic than powders), ready-made pastry dough, or bases and mixes for homemade pizzas.

7

The pantry is the backbone of a busy person's kitchen. Keeping it well stocked means having everything you need to make an impromptu meal, rustle up a snack, or bake a batch of muffins in minutes. Ingredients in the pantry can lift an ordinary meal, add to a ready-prepared meal, or form the basis of an entire meal with just one or two fresh ingredients added.

8

Delegate or let others help; don't try to do it all yourself. Even if it's doing the dishes, setting the table, or making drinks.

9

Make as much as you can in advance and store in the freezer. This will save hours, and having a well-stocked freezer is an entertaining security blanket. Things like soups, stews, ice cream, bread, butter and milk are handy standbys. Make notes to yourself on thawing times and when to take things out of the freezer.

10

ENJOY YOURSELF— don't make things difficult, just follow these rules. This will help your friends to relax as well. Entertaining your friends should be a pleasure.

party food

These delicious crisp cookies are made in minutes. Store them uncooked in the freezer ready to pop into the oven at a moment's notice. Use 2 tablespoons olive oil instead of butter in the dough for a lighter result.

parmesan and rosemary palmiers

4 tablespoons unsalted butter, softened

2 tablespoons chopped fresh rosemary

3 tablespoons freshly grated Parmesan cheese

2 sheets of ready-rolled frozen puff pastry dough, 8 inches square, thawed

coarse sea salt crystals

2 baking sheets, either nonstick or lined with parchment paper

Makes about 40

Put the butter, rosemary, and half the Parmesan cheese in a bowl and mix well. Spread thinly over the squares of pastry dough.

Take one square of dough and roll one edge in towards the middle. Roll the opposite edge in to meet the other one in the middle. Flip over until one roll is on top of the other. Flatten lightly with the palm of your hand. Repeat with the other square of dough. Wrap both rolls separately in plastic wrap and chill or freeze until firm. When ready to bake, remove the wrap and cut each roll into about 20 slices.

Arrange on the baking sheets cut sides down, then sprinkle with the remaining Parmesan and a little coarse salt. Using a rolling pin, lightly roll the cheese and salt into the pastries.

Bake in a preheated oven at 425°F for about 4 minutes on each side until risen and golden brown. Transfer to a wire rack to cool.

Alternatively, open-freeze, then pack in boxes. Bake from frozen in the same way, but for 2–3 minutes longer.

Use only perfectly ripe avocados for this—overripe ones will make the guacamole discolor quickly. To make this go further for larger numbers, stir in ⅔ cup sour cream—it will now serve 6–8 as a dip. Double the quantities to serve more.

the best guacamole
with tortilla chips

2 large ripe avocados

freshly squeezed juice of 2 limes

1 small green chile, seeded and finely chopped

4 scallions, very finely chopped

1 ripe medium tomato, peeled, seeded, and coarsely chopped

2–3 tablespoons coarsely chopped cilantro

sea salt and freshly ground black pepper

tortilla chips or crudités, to serve

Serves 4

Halve the avocados, remove the pits, and scoop out the flesh into a bowl. Mash with a fork to give a coarse texture. Mix in half the lime juice, the chile, scallions, chopped tomato, and cilantro.

Taste and season with salt, pepper, and more lime juice if necessary. Don't make this too far in advance because it will discolor quickly. Cover tightly with plastic wrap, then stir well before serving. Serve with tortilla chips or crudités.

Avocado discoloration It is a myth that leaving an avocado pit in the finished dip will prevent discoloration. No matter what you do, it will discolor in the end. The only thing that works is adding enough lime juice and giving it a quick stir before you put it in the serving dish—and not making it too far in advance.

dukkah

No Egyptian home is complete without a jar of this wonderful seed and nut mixture in the pantry. It is normally eaten as a snack—bread is dipped first into olive oil, then into the dukkah. I like to serve it with grissini and the most delicious olive oil that I can find. It is also great used as a coating for chicken or fish instead of bread crumbs.

1 cup hazelnuts

⅔ cup almonds

⅓ cup sesame seeds

½ cup coriander seeds

½ cup ground cumin

1 teaspoon sea salt

½ teaspoon freshly ground black pepper

To serve

extra virgin olive oil

grissini or strips of toasted flatbread

Makes about 3½ cups

Put the hazelnuts, almonds, and sesame seeds in an ovenproof dish in a preheated oven at 400°F and toast for 5–10 minutes. Remove from the oven, then tip onto a plate to cool completely. If they aren't cool enough, they will turn oily when ground.

Toast the coriander seeds in a dry skillet for 1–2 minutes until you can smell the aroma, tip onto the cooling nuts, then add the ground cumin to the pan. Toast for 30 seconds then transfer to the plate. When cold, put the nuts, spices, salt, and pepper in a food processor and blend to a coarse, powdery meal—still dry-looking, but not totally pulverized. Spoon into a bowl and serve on a tray with a bowl of olive oil and the grissini.

oven-roasted spiced nuts

This recipe gives you control of the salt, the type of nut, and the spice mix. When cool, mix in anything else you fancy, such as dried fruits or seeds.

3 tablespoons unsalted butter

1 tablespoon Indian garam masala, Chinese five-spice, Cajun, or another spice mix, hot or mild

1 egg white

1 lb. mixed blanched nuts, such as almonds, Brazils, hazelnuts, and pecans

1 teaspoon fine sea salt

Makes about 1 lb.

Melt the butter in a small saucepan and stir in the spices. Cool slightly, then whisk in the egg white until foamy. Add the nuts and toss well to coat. Spread out the nuts evenly in a thin layer in a roasting pan and roast slowly in a preheated oven at 300°F for 30 minutes to 1 hour, stirring from time to time, until they are golden and toasted. Remove from the oven and toss the nuts with the salt.

Let cool completely, then store for at least 1 day before eating. They will keep in an airtight container for up to 2 weeks.

There is something quite magnificent about serving a whole fish, simply decorated with pale green cucumber "scales." It is very impressive and so easy—my way of cooking the fish keeps it wonderfully moist, with no chance of overcooking or damaging the fish. A fish kettle is a good investment if you have regular access to fresh salmon and trout.

1 large salmon, about 3 lb., scaled and gutted through the gills if possible

whole poached salmon
with sweet and sour pickled cucumber

Cucumber salad

2 large cucumbers

1 tablespoon sea salt

1 tablespoon sugar

½ cup white wine or cider vinegar

2 tablespoons chopped fresh dill

freshly ground white pepper

Court bouillon

6 cups water

1 tablespoon sea salt

⅔ cup white wine

1 onion, sliced

2 celery stalks, sliced

1 carrot, sliced

a handful of parsley stalks

2 bay leaves

1 teaspoon black peppercorns

To serve

thick homemade mayonnaise

wasabi paste (optional)

extra chopped dill

a fish kettle or large roasting pan

Serves 6

To make the cucumber salad, peel the cucumber, and slice as thinly as possible with a mandoline or in a food processor. Spread in a colander and sprinkle with salt, mixing well. Stand the colander on a plate and leave to disgorge for 30 minutes. Rinse well and squeeze the excess moisture out of the cucumber. Spread the slices over a large plate. Dissolve the sugar in the vinegar and stir in the dill. Pour the mixture over the cucumber and let marinate for at least 1 hour before serving. Grind over lots of white pepper before serving with the salmon.

Put all the court bouillon ingredients in a large saucepan, bring to a boil, and simmer for 1 hour. Let cool completely, then strain the liquid into a fish kettle. Lay the salmon on the rack of the fish kettle and lower into the liquid. The liquid must cover the fish; if not, top up with a little water. Bring slowly to a boil, then cover and turn off the heat. Let cool completely in the liquid. When completely cold, lift out and drain the fish, then remove the skin and slide onto a serving dish. Use the cucumber to cover the salmon with "scales," serving any remaining cucumber separately. Sprinkle with dill and serve with thick homemade mayonnaise flavored with a dash of Japanese wasabi paste, if using.

If serving hot, bring the liquid to a boil, lower the heat to a bare simmer, and poach the salmon for 4 minutes per pound (12 minutes for a 3 lb. salmon). Remove the fish from the liquid, carefully pull off and the skin, and serve with melted butter or hollandaise.

We've had great fun cooking this in the open air over a wood fire, just as they do in Spain, but you can also use a portable gas burner. Paella is the perfect dish for outdoor parties—everything can be prepared ahead of time, then you just add the ingredients in a steady stream until the whole thing comes together. The smell is wonderfully enticing, so make enough for second servings.

a fabulous paella

3 tablespoons good olive oil

6 chicken thighs

6 oz. chorizo sausage, cut into chunks

2 garlic cloves, finely chopped

1 large onion, finely chopped

1 large red bell pepper, finely sliced

2½ cups Spanish paella rice

¾ cup dry white wine

a good pinch of red pepper flakes

2 teaspoons sweet Spanish paprika

about 5 cups chicken stock

a large pinch of saffron strands, soaked in 3 tablespoons hot water

6 ripe tomatoes, quartered

12 whole uncooked shrimp, in their shells

1 lb. fresh mussels, scrubbed, rinsed, and debearded

1 cup fresh or frozen peas

¼ cup chopped fresh flat-leaf parsley

sea salt and freshly ground black pepper

wedges of lime or lemon, to serve

Serves 6

Heat the olive oil in a paella pan or large, deep skillet. Add the chicken thighs and chorizo and brown all over, turning frequently. Stir in the garlic, onion, and bell pepper and cook for about 5 minutes until softened.

Stir in the rice until all the grains are coated and glossy. Add the wine and let it bubble and reduce until almost disappeared. Stir in the red pepper flakes, paprika, chicken stock, and soaked saffron. Stir well, bring to a boil, and simmer gently for 10 minutes.

Stir in the tomatoes and shrimp and cook gently for 5 minutes before finally tucking the mussels into the rice and adding the peas. Cook for another 5 minutes until the mussels open (take out any that do not open after this time). At this stage, almost all the liquid will have been absorbed and the rice will be tender.

Sprinkle the chopped parsley over the top and serve immediately, straight from the pan with a big pile of lime or lemon wedges on the side. This is messy food, so have plenty of paper napkins around.

Cooking mussels Live mussels keep well in a cool place (not the refrigerator), but you can also cook them beforehand. Choose a saucepan with a tight-fitting lid. Heat it dry, then tip in the cleaned mussels. Add the wine, put on the lid and cook for about 5 minutes until the mussels open. Do not overcook, and discard any that don't open. Drain in a colander set over a bowl, let cool, and reserve both the mussels and their cooking liquid. (This can be done well in advance and chilled.) Add the mussel liquid to the paella at the same time as the wine, then add the mussels at the end to heat through.

This makes a beautiful centerpiece on a table—especially when arranged on a large platter. It needs nothing more than a cold noodle salad (page 98) to transform it into a feast for a summer party. Everything can be prepared ahead (even the day before) to be assembled at the last moment.

fillet of beef salad
with thai dressing

1½ lb. piece of beef tenderloin, from the thin end

2 tablespoons olive oil

6 oz. fine green beans, trimmed

3 large hard-cooked eggs

about 8 inches cucumber, peeled and cut into long wedges

8 oz. ripe tomatoes, quartered

½ cup small wrinkled black olives

a handful of fresh basil leaves, torn

freshly ground black pepper

Beef marinade

2 tablespoons freshly squeezed lime juice

2 tablespoons olive oil

2 garlic cloves, crushed

sea salt and freshly ground black pepper

Thai dressing

2 tablespoons fish sauce

3 tablespoons freshly squeezed lime juice

2 tablespoons light soy sauce

1 tablespoon sweet chile sauce

3 tablespoons chopped fresh cilantro

Serves 4

To prepare the marinade, mix the lime juice, the olive oil, garlic, salt, and pepper in a non-metal dish. Add the beef and toss to coat. Cover and let marinate in the refrigerator for 1 hour.

To cook the beef, heat another 2 tablespoons olive oil in a heavy roasting pan or frying pan on top of the stove until smoking. Lift the beef out of the marinade, pat dry, and sear well all over until nicely browned. Transfer to a preheated oven at 400°F and roast for 15–18 minutes for medium rare. Remove from the oven and transfer the beef to a plate to cool.

To make the dressing, put the fish sauce, lime juice, soy sauce, chile sauce, and cilantro in a bowl, whisk well, then set aside to infuse.

Bring a saucepan of salted water to a boil, add the beans, and blanch for 4 minutes. Drain, refresh in cold water, then set aside.

Peel the eggs and cut them in fourths. Heat the dressing and keep it warm. Toss the beans, cucumber, tomatoes, and olives with half the dressing and pile on a serving platter.

Cut the beef in slices and lay them on top of the vegetables. Dot the eggs all around, strew with the basil, spoon over the remaining dressing, and grind pepper on top before serving.

moroccan butterflied grilled lamb

4 lb. leg of lamb

1 tablespoon black peppercorns

1 tablespoon coriander seeds

1 tablespoon cumin seeds

1 tablespoon sweet paprika

2 teaspoon dried thyme

sea salt

freshly squeezed juice of 1 lime

2 garlic cloves, crushed

½ cup plain yogurt

To serve

broiled flatbreads

salad

plain yogurt mixed with chopped fresh mint

Serves 6–8

Moroccan lamb is one of the best and easiest meat dishes for a big barbecue party. Butterflied lamb is just a leg of lamb that has been split open and the bones removed so that it is flat and an even thickness. A butcher will do this for you, although it is quite easy to do yourself. After marinating, the leg can be cooked like one huge steak in much less time than cooking a whole leg, and is so easy to carve for large numbers.

Trim any excess fat off the lamb and score the meat where necessary to make it all the same thickness. Make deep slits all over the meat.

Put the peppercorns, coriander and cumin seeds, and paprika in a dry skillet, toast for a couple of minutes until aromatic, then grind or crush them. Transfer to a bowl, add the thyme, salt to taste, lime juice, garlic, and yogurt and rub all over the cut side of the meat. Put in a shallow dish, cover, and let marinate in the refrigerator for at least 1 hour.

To grill, cook the lamb skin side down over medium-hot coals for 10–12 minutes for medium rare, then turn it over and cook for a further 10–12 minutes. (For medium, cook for a total of 30–35 minutes, and for a total of 40 minutes for well done.)

To broil, put the lamb on a foil-lined rack under a medium-hot broiler for 20 minutes, then turn it over and continue for a further 20 minutes (the meat should be medium).

When cooked, remove from the heat, cover loosely with aluminum foil, and set aside in a warm place to rest for 10 minutes. Carve into long, thin slices. Serve with broiled pita breads, salad, and minted yogurt.

To butterfly a leg of lamb, find the place where the longest bone running down the length of the leg appears to be quite close to the skin. Using a small, sharp knife, slit through the thin surface along that bone and carefully cut the meat back from either side. Work around the bones at the thick end to release the meat, so it opens up like a book and you can lift them out. Open out the meat, skin side down—it should vaguely resemble the wings of a butterfly.

This hearty dish from southwest France is a firm family favorite. It is big and filling, and traditionally made with a type of haricot bean known as *lingots*. However, I adore lima beans for their creamy texture, so that's what I use— feel free to differ. All the components of the dish can be made days in advance, then assembled on the day. It reheats very well (top up with a little more liquid if it looks dry) and is a boon for entertaining vast numbers without fuss. Make this for large gatherings on cold winter days.

a big pot of cassoulet

4 cups dried lima beans, or other white beans

1 lb. smoked Italian pancetta or slab bacon, in a piece

¼ cup olive oil

4 boneless duck breasts, halved crosswise, or chicken legs or thighs

1½ lb. fresh Toulouse sausages or Italian coarse pork sausages, cut into 3 pieces each

2 medium onions, chopped

1 large carrot, chopped

4–6 large garlic cloves, crushed

3 bay leaves

2 teaspoons dried thyme

2 whole cloves

3 tablespoons tomato purée

12 sun-dried tomatoes in oil, drained and coarsely chopped

1½ cups fresh white bread crumbs (ciabatta is good)

4 tablespoons butter

sea salt and freshly ground black pepper

Serves 6–8

The night before, put the beans in a very large bowl, cover with plenty of cold water (to cover them by their depth again), and let soak for several hours.

The next day, drain the beans well and tip into a large saucepan. Cover with fresh water, bring to a boil, then simmer for about 1 hour or until just cooked. Drain well (reserving the cooking liquid).

Trim and discard the rind from the pancetta, then cut the flesh into large pieces. Heat 2 tablespoons of the oil in a skillet, brown the pieces in batches, and transfer to a plate. Heat the remaining oil in the pan, add the duck breasts, and sauté skin side down until the skin is golden. Transfer to the same plate as the pancetta. Brown the sausages in the same way and add to the plate. Add the onions to the pan, then the carrot, garlic, bay leaves, dried thyme, cloves, tomato purée, and sun-dried tomatoes. Cook for 5 minutes until softening.

To assemble the dish, put half the beans in a large, deep casserole dish. Add an even layer of all the meats, then the onion and tomato mixture. Season well with salt and pepper. Cover with the remaining beans, then add enough reserved hot cooking liquid until the beans are almost covered. Sprinkle evenly with bread crumbs and dot with butter. Bake the cassoulet in a preheated oven at 350°F for about 1 hour until a golden crust has formed. Serve warm straight out of the dish.

mexican pork and beans
in red chile sauce

1 medium onion, coarsely chopped

4 garlic cloves, coarsely chopped

1 red bell pepper, halved, seeded, and coarsely chopped

1 fresh fat red chile, seeded and chopped

2 teaspoons mild chili powder

1 teaspoon sweet paprika

1 teaspoon ground cumin

1 teaspoon ground coriander

½ teaspoon cinnamon

1 teaspoon dried oregano

1¼ cups lager beer

1 lb. pork or beef steak

¼ cup safflower oil

14 oz. (2 cups) canned chopped tomatoes

1½ cups tomato juice or passata (Italian puréed, sieved tomatoes)

1 oz. very dark chocolate, chopped

14 oz. (2 cups) canned pinto beans or black-eyed peas, drained and rinsed

sea salt and freshly ground black pepper

To serve

soft tortillas

tomato salsa

chopped avocado

sour cream

Green Rice (page 102)

Serves 4–6

This is my version of chili—not too spicy, made with pork not beef, and just a few beans, then enriched Mexican-style with a little chocolate for depth. Serve it with generous bowls of a simple tomato, cilantro, and onion salsa, chopped cucumber in sour cream, a pile of warm tortillas, and a big bowl of green rice for a great family feast. This is even better made the day before and it freezes very well. For vegetarians, leave out the meat and add cubed and roasted eggplant and quartered mushrooms.

Put the onion, garlic, bell pepper, chile, chili powder, paprika, cumin, coriander, cinnamon, and oregano in a blender or food processor. Add half the lager and blend to a smooth purée.

Trim the steaks, then cut into large pieces. Working in batches, heat the oil in a large saucepan, add the pork, and sauté until browned. Transfer to a plate.

Add the purée to the pan and cook, stirring continuously, over moderate heat for 5 minutes—make sure it doesn't catch and burn, but it should start to caramelize. Stir in the remaining lager, tomatoes, tomato juice, the pork, and juices. Season with salt and pepper and bring to a boil. Reduce the heat and simmer very gently, half-covered, for 30–35 minutes until the pork is tender and the sauce thickened. Stir in the chocolate and beans and heat through.

Serve with the tortillas, salsa, avocado, sour cream, and green rice.

brunch
and snacks

gorgeous granola

Packed with nutty goodness, this cereal is low in sugar and has no added salt. The best way to eat it is with a good dollop of yogurt, a pile of blueberries and raspberries, and some maple syrup. We should all being eating more seeds, nuts, and grains and this mix knocks the spots off anything sold in natural food stores. I have never liked breakfast cereals, but I can eat this in handfuls.

3½ cups rolled oats

1⅓ cups dried shredded coconut

1 cup chopped dried dates, cranberries, or blueberries

¾ cup pumpkin seeds

¾ cup safflower seeds

¾ cup sesame seeds

¾ cup flaxseed

1 cup chopped pecans or almonds, macadamias, Brazils, or other nuts

2 roasting pans

Makes about 10 cups

Spread out the oats in the roasting pans and toast in a preheated oven at 400°F for 15–20 minutes, stirring frequently, until golden brown. Remove and let cool. Mix with all the other ingredients and store in an airtight container.

Variation   For those who like to add sugar, stir ⅔ cup firmly packed brown sugar or ½ cup maple syrup into the oats before toasting. The sugar will melt onto the oats and give a crunch. The maple syrup will make the oats clump together in crunchy nodules.

overnight oatmeal

If you are lucky enough to have a slow-cooker or, even better, an Aga, then this is for you. Your breakfast will be waiting for you in the morning. Oatmeal cooked slowly overnight develops the flavor of the grain and makes it really creamy. There's nothing better on a cold winter's morning to warm your tummy. I like to stir in fresh dates before eating. To make less, just adjust the ingredients, but the cooking time will be the same.

3 cups steel-cut oats

sea salt

cold milk or cream, honey, and fruit, to serve (optional)

a slow-cooker (optional)

Serves 8

Just before going to bed, bring 7 cups cold water to a boil in a large saucepan. Add 2 teaspoons salt. Shower in the oatmeal, whisking all the time. Return to a boil and boil for 1 minute.

Either pour into a casserole dish, cover with the lid, and put in a slow oven at 275°F or the Aga. Alternatively, put in the bowl of a preheated slow-cooker, cover with the lid, and cook on LOW.

Cook for about 8 hours or overnight. The oatmeal will be ready the next day—you will have to remove a skin from the top and probably add a little boiling water to thin it down. Serve with cold milk or cream, honey, and any fruit you like.

tea-infused fruit compote

Keep a big bowl of this compote in the refrigerator—it keeps well and is great with yogurt and a sprinkling of seeds. With lighter teas, use lighter-flavored fruits such as peaches and apples and flavor with lemon zest. Use orange zest to flavor stronger teas, together with stronger spices such as star anise. There is no need to add sugar, because the natural sugars from the fruits thicken the syrup as it cooks.

2 teaspoons leaf tea, such as Earl Grey, jasmine, or other tea

1 lb. mixed dried fruit, such as prunes, apricots, figs, or others

1¼ cups apple juice

2 crushed cardamom pods

1 cinnamon stick

thinly peeled zest of 1 unwaxed orange

Serves 4

Make a large pot of tea with the leaf tea and 1 quart boiling water and set aside to brew. Put the fruit in a bowl and completely cover with the brewed tea. Cover and let soak for several hours or overnight.

Transfer to a saucepan, then add the apple juice, cardamom pods, cinnamon stick, and orange zest. Bring slowly to a boil, then reduce the heat and simmer for about 20 minutes until soft. Remove all the spices and let cool.

Cover and chill in the refrigerator. This will keep for a week in the refrigerator, and can be frozen.

swiss muesli

After tasting this on a skiing holiday in Switzerland, I can't think why anyone would eat commercial breakfast cereal again. Soaking the oats in apple juice (or other juice) overnight transforms them from dry and dusty to light and flavorsome. The finer the oats, the smoother the texture. Delicious with creamy plain yogurt stirred in.

1 cup porridge oats, rolled oats, or oat flakes

1⅓ cups large raisins or other dried fruit

2⅔ cups apple juice

1½ cups plain yogurt

4 apples, grated or chopped

4 bananas or a mixture of seasonal fruit

4 oranges, peeled and segmented or chopped

honey, to taste

Makes 4 large portions

Put the oats and raisins in a bowl and pour over the apple juice. Cover and let soak in the refrigerator overnight.

The next day, stir in the yogurt, then add more fruit juice and honey to taste. Stir in half the fruit and sprinkle the remainder on top.

bacon and eggs in a pan

A whole breakfast made without fuss in one pan. Use the best bacon you can find and fresh free-range eggs. It's made like a giant omelet—almost an Italian frittata. Serve in wedges.

1 tablespoon safflower oil

8 slices bacon

6 extra-large eggs

10 cherry tomatoes, halved

2 tablespoons snipped fresh chives

sea salt and freshly ground black pepper

Serves 4

Heat a large, preferably nonstick skillet, about 9 inches diameter, over medium heat. Add 1 tablespoon safflower oil, heat, then add the bacon. Cook for 2 minutes until it is beginning to brown and crisp around the edges.

Break the eggs into a bowl, add salt and pepper, and whisk lightly. Pour into the skillet around the bacon, making sure the base is covered and the bacon sits half-submerged. Dot with the tomatoes and cook over medium to low heat until the eggs have set. Sprinkle with chives and serve immediately, cut into wedges.

fearless scrambled eggs

Scrambled eggs should be lovely and creamy, not watery grey lumps. You cannot make these in advance, just wait until everyone is around and cook them in seconds. I use a non-stick saucepan and a spurtle (wooden porridge stirrer, often with a thistle handle), but a wooden spoon or spatula will do. Eat them as soon as they are cooked—they do not hang around.

6 extra-large very fresh free-range eggs

3 tablespoons milk or cream

4 tablespoons unsalted butter

3 tablespoons chopped fresh parsley

sea salt and freshly ground black pepper

buttered toasted English muffins, to serve

Serves 4

Put the eggs, milk, and a pinch of salt and pepper in a bowl and whisk until smooth. Melt the butter in a nonstick saucepan until foaming. Pour in the eggs and cook over medium heat until they start to set on the base of the pan (use the spoon to scrape the bottom to check). Cook them, stirring slowly but constantly, and scraping the bottom and sides of the pan to mix in the cooking eggs. Continue scraping, mixing and stirring, until the eggs thicken and start to look like lumpy but creamy custard. Add salt and pepper to taste, then stir in the parsley. Spoon onto toasted muffins and serve immediately.

Variations
• Stir in chopped smoked salmon or other smoked fish just before the eggs are ready.
• Cook 3 chopped scallions in the butter, add a little chopped fresh ginger and a little chopped fresh chile, stir in ½ teaspoon curry powder and a couple of chopped tomatoes, and cook until soft. Add the eggs and cook as above, stirring in 2 tablespoons chopped fresh cilantro at the last moment. Serve immediately.

sausage and bacon rolls

There's nothing quite like a warm sausage-filled roll for brunch. Dotting the sausages with mustard and wrapping them in bacon just adds to the taste experience and the cooking smells will waken even the most hung-over. Get these under way while you make juice and tea or coffee.

16 thin slices Italian pancetta or bacon

a little mustard (any kind)

8 all-meat fresh sausages

olive oil, for brushing

To serve

4 warm buttered soft rolls or pita bread

tomato ketchup or broiled tomatoes

Serves 4

Preheat the broiler to medium. Spread a little mustard over each slice of bacon. Wrap 2 slices around each sausage. Put the sausages on the rack of a broiler pan so that the loose ends of the bacon are underneath the sausage. Brush with a little oil and broil for 6–8 minutes on each side, depending on the thickness of the sausage, until the bacon is crisp and the sausage cooked through. Serve in buttered rolls with plenty of tomato ketchup or broiled tomatoes.

nut butter on toast

Homemade nut butter is SO much better than bought peanut butter, and most impressive, taking seconds to make. You can use blanched nuts, but I like to leave the skins on. You can mix two or three varieties together for a more sophisticated taste, but make sure they are very fresh—stale nuts will make nasty butter. If too rich, you can add a few tablespoons tahini paste to the nuts before grinding.

2 cups safflower oil

4 oz. shelled nuts, such as Brazils, cashews, almonds, hazelnuts, or walnuts

a pinch of salt

Makes about 2¾ cups

Pour the oil into a blender or food processor with a sharp blade (a blender will give a smoother result). Add the nuts and a pinch of salt. Pulse in short bursts, scraping down the sides every now and then to make it blend evenly. Taste, adding extra salt if necessary. Pack into screwtop jars and store in a cold place or in the refrigerator.

Use this basic mixture to create different kinds of muffins. If you prepare the dry mix the day before, you can quickly rustle up some muffins first thing in the morning.

muffin mania

1⅔ cups all-purpose flour
⅔ cup sugar
1 tablespoon baking powder
½ teaspoon sea salt
1 extra-large egg
½ cup milk (or a little more)
¼ cup safflower oil

a 6- or 12-cup muffin pan, greased with butter
paper liners (see tip)

Makes 12 small or 6 large muffins

Preheat the oven to 350°F. Sift the flour, sugar, baking powder, and salt together into a large bowl or plastic bag.

Whisk the egg in a large bowl, then beat in the milk and oil. Add the dry ingredients and stir until just blended. The mixture should look very coarse with lumps and floury pockets.

Spoon into the prepared muffin pan, filling three-quarters full. Bake for about 20 minutes or until well risen and golden brown.

Remove from the oven and turn the tray upside down onto a cooling rack. Leave for 2 minutes for the steam to loosen the muffins. Lift off the tray and turn the muffins the right way up. Serve warm—they do not reheat well.

Variations
• Experiment with different flours, and adjust the liquid accordingly because whole-wheat flours tend to absorb more liquid.
• Add nuts, seeds, and dried fruits to the basic mixture.
• Use light brown sugar instead of white sugar.
• Sift in spices with the dry ingredients.
• Quickly stir whole berries or chopped fresh fruit into the batter before baking.
• For a crunchy topping, mix chopped nuts and seeds into light brown sugar and sprinkle on top of the muffins before baking.

Tip Put a paper liner in each muffin cup and they will never stick.

soups and appetizers

This isn't so difficult to make—and very impressive. I like to use smoked salmon fillet for this (sometimes known as royal fillet). It is very meaty and you can cut it to the size you want. It may not be truly authentic, but it is great served with drinks on a hot summer's night. The uncut rolls can be wrapped up tightly in plastic wrap, then cut and unwrapped at the last moment to preserve the freshness.

smoked salmon and cucumber sushi rolls

scant 2 cups Japanese sushi rice

2 tablespoons sugar

1 teaspoon sea salt

¼ cup rice wine vinegar

1 large cucumber, unwaxed if possible

5 sheets dried nori seaweed

8 oz. sliced smoked salmon

3 teaspoons wasabi paste

To serve
Japanese pickled ginger

Japanese soy sauce, such as tamari

wasabi paste

sushi mat or clean cloth

Serves 6

Put the rice in a strainer and wash well under running water until the water runs clear. Drain well and tip into a saucepan. Add 2¾ cups water and bring to a boil. Boil fast for 5 minutes, reduce the heat, cover, and cook slowly for 10 minutes until all the water has been absorbed.

Meanwhile, put the sugar, salt, and vinegar in a bowl and stir until dissolved. Tip the cooked rice onto a plate or tray and sprinkle with the vinegar mixture. Mix lightly with your hands, then let cool.

Cut the cucumber into long strips the length of the long side of the nori.

To make the sushi rolls, put a sheet of nori shiny side down on a sushi mat or clean cloth. Spread one-fifth of the rice over the nori, leaving a clear strip down one long edge. Cover the rice with a thin layer of smoked salmon and spread with a little wasabi paste (thin it down with a little water if you like). Put a cucumber strip along the side opposite the clear strip of seaweed. Dampen the clear end.

Starting from the cucumber end and using the mat to help you, roll up like a jelly roll, sealing it into a secure cylinder with the dampened edge. Using a very sharp knife, cut into 1-inch lengths. Repeat with the remaining seaweed, rice, and salmon. Serve with pickled ginger, soy sauce, and more wasabi for dipping.

These small, spicy, savory jellies are served in glasses with rich and salty tapenade spread on thin toasts. There's a surprise olive hidden in the center of each jelly.

jellied bloody marys
with tapenade toasts

1 envelope powdered gelatin

2¾ cups tomato juice

⅔ cup vodka

freshly squeezed juice of 2 limes or 1 lemon

1 tablespoon Worcestershire sauce

1 teaspoon Tabasco sauce

freshly ground black pepper

celery salt

Quick tapenade

1 cup Greek-style black olives, pitted, plus 6 extra to serve

2 garlic cloves, peeled

3 canned anchovies, drained

2 teaspoons capers, rinsed and drained

1 tablespoon olive oil, plus extra for the jar

1 small baguette loaf, to serve

Serves 6

Put 3 tablespoons water in a very small saucepan, sprinkle with the gelatin, and leave to swell and sponge. Heat gently to dissolve.

Put the tomato juice, vodka, strained lemon juice, Worcestershire sauce, and Tabasco in a pitcher, season generously with black pepper and celery salt, and mix well. Stir in the melted gelatin, mix well, and pour into 6 glasses set on a tray until half full. Refrigerate for 30 minutes until set, but keep the remaining jelly out of the refrigerator to stay liquid. Put an olive on top of each set jelly, spoon over a little liquid jelly, then refrigerate to set and anchor the olive. Finally, fill with the remaining jelly and chill until set and ready to serve.

Meanwhile, to make the tapenade, put the olives, garlic, anchovies, capers, and olive oil in a food processor and blend until smooth. Scrape out into a jar and cover with a layer of olive oil until needed. Cut the baguette into very thin slices and toast on both sides until golden. Spread thinly with the tapenade.

Put a glass of jelly on each plate with a pile of toasts and serve immediately.

This is one of those simple, stunning dishes that is divine and addictive. You pull the garlic apart with your fingers and squeeze the golden purée onto each mouthful of bruschetta as you go. Try to use goat cheese with a rind because it will help contain the cheese while it's melting under the broiler.

broiled goat cheese and rosemary bruschetta
with baked garlic cloves

4 thick slices of country bread, preferably sourdough

2 garlic cloves, peeled and bruised

extra virgin olive oil

¼ cup basil pesto (page 64)

8 thick slices goat cheese with rind, such as Bucheron chèvre

sea salt and freshly ground black pepper

Baked garlic

4 large heads of garlic

¾ cup olive oil, heated

4 sprigs of thyme

2–3 sprigs of rosemary

sea salt and freshly ground black pepper

Serves 4

To prepare the garlic, slice off the top third of each bulb. Pack cut side up in a small baking dish, pour over the olive oil, and tuck in the thyme and a couple of rosemary sprigs. Season well with salt and pepper and bake in a preheated oven at 325°F for about 1 hour until meltingly soft.

Remove the garlic from the oven and let cool until warm.

Meanwhile, grill, toast, or pan-grill the bread on one side only until lightly charred or toasted, rub each cooked side with the bruised garlic, then sprinkle with oil. Keep it warm.

Spread the pesto over the ungrilled side of the bruschetta and put 2 slices of cheese on each one. Sprinkle with salt and pepper, then cook under a hot broiler for 1–2 minutes or until the cheese is beginning to melt and color (watch that the bread doesn't start to burn).

Pull the garlic cloves apart and serve a few cloves on top of each bruschetta with a little more oil. Squeeze out the soft garlic and spread onto the bruschetta, then serve.

Normally this dish is made from eggplant that have been roasted whole and the flesh scooped out. In this version, I peel off the skin first, then slice and roast in the oven, so the result is much more mellow. This creamy dip can be part of a selection of meze dishes served as an informal appetizer.

baba ghanoush

2 lb. eggplant

about ⅔ cup olive oil

2 garlic cloves, crushed

¼ cup tahini (sesame seed paste)

freshly squeezed juice of 1–2 lemons, or to taste

sea salt and freshly ground black pepper

To serve

1 tablespoon sweet paprika

3 tablespoons olive oil

2 tablespoon chopped fresh flat leaf parsley

pita bread or other flatbread

a baking sheet

Serves 4–6

Trim the eggplant, peel, then slice thickly. Arrange the pieces on a baking sheet and brush both sides with olive oil. Roast in a preheated oven at 400°F for about 20 minutes until browning and soft, turning them at least once.

Remove from the oven and let cool for 5 minutes. Transfer to a food processor and add the garlic, tahini, and the juice of 1 lemon. Process until creamy, then taste and adjust the seasoning with salt, pepper, and more lemon juice.

Pour or spoon into a shallow dish. Mix the paprika with the 3 tablespoons olive oil and trickle it over the top of the baba ghanoush. Sprinkle with parsley and serve with pita bread for dipping.

Note For a softer garlic flavor, roast the garlic cloves whole and unpeeled with the eggplant, then squeeze the soft flesh out of the skins and blend into the eggplant.

To cook eggplant in the microwave, prick 2 medium eggplant all over with the point of a sharp knife. This will stop them exploding in the oven. Line the turntable of the microwave with a double layer of paper towels and put the eggplant on top. Microwave on HIGH for about 12 minutes (for 1 lb.) or until collapsed and completely soft. Cut open and scoop out the flesh. This will make a lighter, sharper dip.

This exceptionally smooth, creamy pâté makes an impressive appetizer, especially when served with toasted brioche and a sharp, fruity chutney to cut the richness. The parfait can also be set in individual pots, and I would pour a layer of melted unsalted butter on top to seal them.

chicken liver parfait
with bitter orange and onion chutney

1 lb. chicken livers, fresh or frozen and thawed

1½ sticks unsalted butter, softened

2 shallots, peeled and finely chopped

scant ½ cup cognac, Armagnac, or Madeira

scant ½ cup heavy cream or crème fraîche

a large pinch of ground mace

a large pinch of allspice

sea salt and freshly ground black pepper

warm toasted brioche or char-grilled bread, to serve

Bitter orange and onion chutney

3 unwaxed oranges

14 oz. red onions, peeled and chopped

1 tart apple, about 6 oz., peeled, cored, and chopped

1 cup chunky dark orange marmalade

½ cup firmly packed dark brown sugar

1¼ cups cider or white wine vinegar

sea salt and freshly ground black pepper

a loaf pan, 8 x 4 inches, lined with plastic wrap

Serves 4–6: makes 2¾ cups chutney

Trim the chicken livers, discarding the white fibrous parts and any discolored areas.

Melt 2 tablespoons butter in a skillet, add the shallots, and cook gently for 1–2 minutes until beginning to soften. Increase the heat slightly and add the livers. Turn them in the pan for 2–3 minutes until just browned and "seized," but still soft and pink on the inside. Tip into a blender. Deglaze the pan with the cognac, scraping up any sediment. Boil to reduce by half, then add to the blender. Add the cream, plenty of salt and pepper, then the mace and allspice. Blend until smooth. Add the remaining butter and blend again until smooth. Push the mixture through a fine-mesh strainer and check the seasoning. Spoon into the prepared loaf pan and level the surface. Cool, then refrigerate for several hours or overnight until firm.

Meanwhile, to make the chutney, peel the oranges. Finely shred or chop the rind of 1 orange and discard the remaining rind. Chop the flesh of the oranges and put into a non-reactive saucepan. Add the onions, apples, marmalade, sugar, vinegar, salt, and pepper. Bring to a boil, then simmer for about 1 hour, stirring every now and then until very thick and pulpy. Spoon into a jar, seal, and cool. This will keep in the refrigerator for at least a month.

To serve, turn out the parfait, remove the plastic wrap, and cut into slices with a warm knife. Serve with warm toasted brioche or grilled bread and a large spoonful of chutney.

1½ lb. fresh ripe tomatoes, cored and quartered

1¼ cups tomato or V8 juice

1 small garlic clove, peeled and crushed

1 medium red bell pepper, halved,
seeded, and coarsely chopped

2 scallions, trimmed and coarsely chopped

1 cucumber, peeled and coarsely chopped

2 tablespoons chopped cilantro

2 tablespoons sherry vinegar

1 tablespoon sweet chile sauce

sea salt and freshly ground black pepper

Frozen vegetable cubes

3 tablespoons finely chopped cucumber

3 tablespoons finely chopped red bell pepper

3 tablespoons finely chopped radishes

3 tablespoons finely chopped tomato

Serves 6

I add jewel-like cubes of frozen finely chopped vegetables to the soup instead of the usual blocks of watery ice cubes.

jeweled gazpacho

Put the tomatoes and juice in a blender and blend until smooth. Pour half into a pitcher. Mix all the remaining vegetables in a bowl. Add half the vegetables to the blender, blend again until smooth, and transfer to a bowl. Put the tomato mixture, the remaining vegetables, and the cilantro in the blender, blend until smooth, then add to the bowl. Stir well, then mix in the vinegar, chile sauce, and salt and pepper to taste. Cover and chill overnight.

To make the frozen vegetable cubes, mix the chopped vegetables together and pack into ice-cube trays. Freeze.

Ladle the soup into chilled bowls or tumblers and put a couple of frozen vegetable cubes in each one.

This is a deliciously smooth and velvety soup that will suit all tastes and any occasion, from picnics to dinner parties. To ensure a really smooth texture, it is very important to blend, then strain the soup before serving hot or chilled.

leek and potato soup
with watercress purée

5½ tablespoons unsalted butter

2 medium onions, thinly sliced

1 lb. leeks (white part only), thinly sliced

1 medium potato, chopped

5½ cups chicken stock

1¼ cups milk

⅔ cup sour cream or crème fraîche, plus extra to serve

sea salt and freshly ground white pepper

Watercress purée

1 cup watercress leaves, washed

⅓ cup good olive oil

Serves 6

To make the purée, put the watercress leaves in a blender with the olive oil. Blend until smooth. Pour into a screwtop jar and set aside.

To make the soup, melt the butter in a large saucepan and add the onions and leeks. Stir well, add 3 tablespoons water, cover tightly, and cook over gentle heat for 10 minutes until soft and golden, but not at all brown.

Stir in the potatoes and chicken stock. Bring to a boil, reduce the heat, cover, and simmer for 20 minutes until the potatoes are tender. Stir in the milk, then purée in a blender or with a hand-held stick blender. Press the purée through a strainer, then return it to the pan. Stir in the sour cream and season with salt and pepper to taste. Cool and chill (if serving chilled, add extra seasoning) or serve hot in warm soup bowls with a swirl of watercress purée and spoonful of chilled sour cream.

chickpea chermoula soup

2 cups dried chickpeas, soaked overnight in water with a pinch of baking soda, or 28 oz. (4 cups) canned chickpeas, drained and rinsed

4 tablespoons unsalted butter or 3 tablespoons olive oil, plus extra to serve

4 oz. chopped Italian pancetta, bacon, prosciutto, or bacon lardons

2 medium onions, finely chopped

1 carrot, chopped

1 celery stalk, chopped

2 garlic cloves, finely chopped

½ teaspoon sweet paprika

½ teaspoon ground cinnamon

½ teaspoon ground ginger

½ teaspoon ground cumin

½ teaspoon dried thyme

14 oz. (2 cups) canned chopped tomatoes

1½ cups prepared baby spinach leaves

1½ cups chopped fresh cilantro

sea salt and freshly ground black pepper

Serves 6

Drain the chickpeas, put in a saucepan, cover with fresh water, and bring to a boil. Cover and simmer for 40 minutes or until tender. Alternatively, used canned chickpeas for a quick version.

Meanwhile, heat the butter in a skillet and add the pancetta, if using. Sauté over medium heat until the fat begins to run. Add the chopped vegetables and garlic and cook for 5–10 minutes until beginning to soften and brown. Stir in the spices and thyme and cook for 1 minute. When cooked, drain the chickpeas, reserve the cooking liquid, and return the pulses to the pan. Stir in the pancetta and vegetables, the tomatoes, and about 1 quart reserved cooking liquid to cover completely. Bring to a boil, partially cover with a lid, reduce the heat, and simmer for 30 minutes, stirring occasionally. The chickpeas should start to disintegrate and thicken the soup. Add salt and pepper to taste, then stir in the spinach and cilantro 5 minutes before serving sprinkled with olive oil.

fiery red bell pepper soup

If making this for children, omit the chiles and use 2 cups milk mixed with 2 cups stock.

6 medium red bell peppers

6 carrots, about 1 lb.

1–2 fresh red chiles (optional)

1½ lb. ripe plum tomatoes

3 large garlic cloves, peeled

⅓ cup olive oil

2 teaspoons smoked sweet paprika (Spanish pimentón dulce)

5 cups vegetable or beef stock

sea salt and freshly ground black pepper

crisply fried bacon slices, to serve

Serves 8: makes 9 cups

Cut the stalk ends off the bell peppers, halve, and scrape out the seeds. Scrape the carrots and cut into chunky fingers.

If using chiles, cut off the stalks, cut in half, and scrape out the seeds (wearing rubber gloves if you like).

Put the bell peppers, carrots, chiles, tomatoes, and garlic in several large roasting pans so the vegetables aren't too cramped, then toss them in the olive oil. Season well with salt and pepper. Roast in a preheated oven at 400°F for about 30 minutes until all the vegetables are soft and slightly charred at the edges.

Transfer half the vegetables to a blender, add the paprika and half the stock, and purée until smooth. Pour into a saucepan and repeat with the remaining vegetables and stock, adding extra stock if it seems too thick. Reheat until almost boiling, add salt and pepper to taste, then serve with the bacon crumbled over the top.

main dishes

Make your own Green Thai Curry Paste (page 136) and keep it in the refrigerator for the best flavor, or buy some the next time you visit an Asian store—it keeps very well.

green shrimp curry
with thin noodles

1 quart fish or vegetable stock

¼ cup Green Thai Curry Paste (page 136)

8 oz. (4 nests) thin stir-fry rice noodles

2 cups canned coconut milk

1½ lb. uncooked peeled shrimp

1½ cups frozen peas

3 tablespoons chopped cilantro

sea salt

To serve

6 scallions, shredded

1 red bell pepper, halved, seeded, and finely shredded

Serves 6

Put 1 cup of the stock and all the curry paste in a sauté pan, whisk well, then bring to a boil. Simmer for 2 minutes until all the liquid has evaporated. Add the remaining stock and stir well. Bring to a boil, reduce the heat, and simmer for 10 minutes.

Meanwhile bring a large saucepan of water to a boil, add the noodles, cover with a lid, remove from the heat, and let soak for 4 minutes. Stir, then drain well.

Pour the coconut milk into the curry sauce, add the shrimp and peas, stir well, and simmer for 5 minutes. Stir in the noodles and cilantro, taste, and season with salt. Serve topped with shredded scallions and bell pepper.

If using tofu, cut into large cubes and sauté on one side for 2 minutes in very hot oil in a nonstick skillet. Turn the pieces over and cook for a further 2 minutes. Add to the curry at the last moment.

I have happy memories of a mussel feast my sister and I cooked for twelve friends many years ago. Everyone pitched in. Lots of willing hands helped scrub the mussels. We set up a trestle table and covered it with a large white bedsheet tablecloth. While the mussels were cooking (and it took some time for such a large volume), the bread was warmed, and much wine flowed. We had borrowed a huge catering pot from a friend and it had to be stirred occasionally by the strongest and bravest. It was one of the best meals I have ever had and it went on for hours. Take the pot to the table and ladle out the mussels first, then serve the delicious soupy juices to be mopped up with crusty bread.

moules marinière feast

6 lb. fresh mussels

¼ cup olive oil

3 garlic cloves, very finely chopped

3 onions, very finely chopped

¾ cup dry white wine

a good pinch of hot red pepper flakes

¼ cup coarsely chopped
fresh flat-leaf parsley

lots of hot French bread, to serve

a large piece of cheesecloth

Serves 6

Scrub the mussels well, knock off any barnacles, and pull off the beards. Discard any broken mussels and any that won't close when they are tapped on the work surface. Drain in a colander.

Heat the oil in a large saucepan. Add the garlic and onions and sauté for 10 minutes until softened but not colored. Add the wine, pepper flakes, and ¾ cup water, bring to a boil, and simmer for another 10 minutes. (This can be done in advance.)

Add the mussels, cover, and cook over high heat for about 5 minutes, shaking the pan every now and then, until the mussels have opened. Discard any that remain closed. Strain the mussels through a cheesecloth-lined colander set over a bowl or saucepan.

Keep the mussels warm in the pan and boil the mussel liquid to reduce slightly. Stir in the chopped parsley. Pile the mussels into warmed bowls and pour over the hot broth. Serve with the bread to mop up the broth.

Marinating salmon concentrates the flavor and gives the steaks a lovely glaze when broiled. Melted pesto makes a wonderful sauce—add more olive oil if you like it thinner and less rich. Although cherry or baby plum tomatoes look and taste great, you can use larger ones chopped to a similar size—just make sure they are properly ripe.

salmon steaks
with hot pesto and tomatoes

4 salmon steaks, 6–8 oz. each

2 tablespoons balsamic vinegar

2 teaspoons soy sauce

12 oz. baby plum tomatoes, halved

extra basil leaves, to serve

Pesto

2 garlic cloves, peeled

½ cup pine nuts

¼ cup freshly grated Parmesan
or aged pecorino cheese

1½ cups fresh basil leaves (no stalks)

⅔ cup extra virgin olive oil

4 tablespoons unsalted butter, softened

sea salt and freshly ground black pepper

Serves 4

Put the salmon steaks in a shallow non-metal dish. Put the balsamic vinegar and soy sauce in a measuring jug, mix well, then pour over the steaks, turning to coat. Cover and let marinate in the refrigerator for 30 minutes.

To make the pesto, put everything in a blender or food processor and purée until as smooth as you like. Store in a jar with a layer of olive oil on top to exclude the air. Keep in the refrigerator until needed, making sure that, each time you use it, you level the surface and re-cover with olive oil.

Remove the salmon from the marinade and put in a foil-lined broiler pan. Cook under a preheated broiler for 4 minutes on each side, brushing with the marinade once on each side. Remove from the broiler and keep warm.

Put the pesto in a saucepan and heat gently until warm and melted. Carefully stir in the tomatoes. Serve the salmon on warm plates with the pesto tomato sauce spooned over, then topped with basil.

Pesto freezes well, so when the best basil is around in the summer, I make and freeze pesto in ice-cube trays, then pop the cubes out into plastic bags. Don't thaw the cubes, just let them melt into whatever's cooking.

If your tomatoes aren't ripe enough, put them on a sunny windowsill or in the fruit bowl for 2–3 days—they will completely change. The refrigerator is death to a tomato.

chicken with forty cloves of garlic

4 lb. free-range organic chicken

2 lemons, sliced

4 sprigs of thyme

a few large sprigs of rosemary

a few sprigs of sage

5 bay leaves

¾ cup olive oil

40 unpeeled fat garlic cloves

3⅓ cups all-purpose flour

sea salt and freshly ground black pepper

12 thin croûtes or toasts, to serve

Serves 4

A great alternative to the Sunday roast is this classic dish from Provence. It uses all the herby flavors of the hot sunny hillside, olive oil, and of course a massive amount of garlic. The long cooking makes the garlic meltingly tender. The chicken is carved and served with the garlic, which is squeezed out of the skins and spread onto crisp toasts.

Season the cavity of the bird with salt and pepper. Add the sliced lemon and 2 sprigs of thyme. Push 2 sprigs of thyme, 2 sprigs of rosemary, 2 sprigs of sage, and 2 bay leaves between the skin and the breast on both sides of the chicken. Pour the olive oil into a casserole dish and turn the chicken around in it to coat it all over. Add the garlic cloves and remaining herbs and mix with the oil to coat. Sprinkle again with salt and pepper.

Mix the flour with enough water to make into a soft dough. Roll the dough into a long cylinder and press it around the edge of the casserole dish. Press the lid down on top and push any overhanging dough over the edge of the lid to seal.

Bake in a preheated oven at 350°F for 1½ hours. By this time, the chicken will be cooked, but will happily sit unopened for 15–20 minutes. Take the dish to the table, crack open the crust, and lift off the lid to release the aroma of Provence.

Carve the chicken or cut it into pieces and serve each portion with the collected juices and a pile of garlic to spread on toasts.

All the flavors of the Tuscan countryside are captured in these little packages. Rosemary and sage grow wild there, and are the most common used in Tuscan cooking. Don't be alarmed at the amount of salt and pepper used—this gives it the authentic punchy flavor. A great dish to prepare ahead and cook at the last moment.

chicken with tuscan herbs

4 garlic cloves

2 teaspoons sea salt

1 teaspoon freshly ground black pepper

3 tablespoons chopped fresh rosemary and sage, mixed

12 boneless skinless free-range chicken thighs

24 black kalamata olives, pitted and chopped

12 thin slices Italian pancetta, prosciutto, or bacon

12 fresh bay leaves

To serve

olive oil

Olive Oil and Parmesan Mash (see note)

fine kitchen twine

Serves 6

Pound the garlic, salt, pepper, and rosemary with a mortar and pestle. Rub the paste generously all over the flesh side of the thighs. Dot with the olives. Reshape the thighs and wrap each one with a slice of pancetta and tuck in a bay leaf. Tie each package in 2 places with fine kitchen twine. (They can be frozen at this stage—remove from the freezer and thaw at room temperature for 2 hours before cooking.)

When ready to cook, arrange the packages on a broiler pan and brush with olive oil. Cook under a preheated broiler for 20 minutes, turning every 5 minutes until golden and crisp and cooked through. Alternatively, bake in a preheated oven at 400°F for 20–25 minutes. Sprinkle with extra olive oil and serve with olive oil and Parmesan mash.

Note Olive Oil and Parmesan Mash
Make the basic recipe for Perfect Mashed Potatoes on page 102. Heat ¼ cup of olive oil with the milk instead of the butter, then beat in ½ cup freshly grated Parmesan.

The tenderloin is the most tender cut of beef and is best cooked until rosy pink inside. Resting the meat before carving will ensure a juicy result.

perfect roast tenderloin of beef
with herbed yorkshire puddings

2 lb. beef tenderloin in a piece (not from the thick end)

olive oil

sea salt and freshly ground black pepper

8 oz. thinly sliced Italian pancetta, prosciutto, or bacon

Herbed Yorkshire puddings

1⅔ cups all-purpose flour

½ teaspoon sea salt

2 large sprigs of rosemary, chopped

1 tablespoon chopped fresh thyme

4 large eggs

2¾ cups milk

8 tablespoons beef dripping, duck fat, or safflower oil

To serve

Vichy Carrots (page 105)

Scallion and Horseradish Mash (page 102)

kitchen twine

a 12-cup muffin pan or Yorkshire pudding pan

Serves 6

To make the Yorkshire puddings, sift the flour and salt into a food processor or blender. Add the rosemary and thyme, eggs, and milk. Blend until smooth and pour into a pitcher. Cover and refrigerate for at least 1 hour.

Trim the fillet of all fat and membrane and neatly tie at regular intervals to give a good shape. Rub all over with olive oil, salt, and pepper. Wrap with the pancetta. Cover and set aside for 20 minutes to return to room temperature.

Put the meat in a roasting pan and cook in a preheated oven at 450°F for 25 minutes for medium rare (20 for very rare, 35 for medium). Remove from the oven, cover loosely with aluminum foil, and let rest in a warm place for 10–15 minutes (this will make it easier to carve and give the meat an even pink color).

Lower the oven temperature to 400°F and cook the puddings while the meat is resting. Put the dripping into the cups of the muffin pan and heat in the oven for a couple of minutes. Stir the batter and pour into the hot pans—the batter should sizzle as soon as it hits the fat. Return to the oven and bake for 15–20 minutes until well-risen and deep golden brown—do not open the oven during cooking.

Carve the meat into chunky slices (3 per person) and serve with the Yorkshire puddings and the juices from the meat. Serve with vegetables such as Vichy carrots and scallion and horseradish mash.

This glorious recipe can be made as a large pie, or as individual pies for a special occasion. It can be completely made ahead of time—even frozen. Make the stew in advance, top with dough, and refrigerate until ready to put in the oven—the individual pies can be cooking while you eat your appetizer. If you don't want to use dough, serve as a stew with plenty of mashed potatoes. Dried wild mushrooms are available in most supermarkets.

steak and wild mushroom pies

2 oz. dried wild mushrooms

⅓ cup olive oil or dripping

1 onion, finely chopped

3 garlic cloves, chopped

1 large carrot, finely chopped

2 celery stalks, finely chopped

4 oz. cubed Italian pancetta, prosciutto, or bacon

8 juniper berries, crushed

3 bay leaves

2 tablespoons chopped fresh thyme

2 tablespoons all-purpose flour

2 lb. stewing beef, trimmed and cut into 1½-inch cubes

1¼ cups red wine

2 tablespoons cranberry or red currant jelly

1 package (17.3 oz) puff pastry sheets

1 large egg, beaten

sea salt and freshly ground black pepper

6 individual pie dishes or 1 large pie dish

2 baking sheets

Serves 6

Put the dried mushrooms in a bowl, just cover with hot water, and let soak for 30 minutes. Meanwhile, heat half the oil in a large casserole dish, add the onion, garlic, carrot, and celery, and cook for 5–10 minutes until softening. Stir in the pancetta and sauté with the vegetables until just beginning to brown. Add the juniper berries, bay leaves, and thyme, sprinkle in the flour, mix well, and set aside.

Heat the remaining olive oil in a large skillet and sauté the beef quickly (in batches) on all sides until crusty and brown. Transfer to the casserole dish as you go. When done, deglaze the skillet with the wine, let bubble, then scrape up the sediment from the bottom of the pan. Pour over the meat and vegetables.

Drain the mushrooms and add to the casserole dish with ⅔ cup of the soaking water and the cranberry jelly. Season very well with salt and pepper, then stir well. Bring to a boil on top of the stove, then simmer for 1½ hours until tender. Let cool overnight.

Next day, spoon the stew into 6 individual pie dishes. Cut out 6 circles of dough, a good 1 inch wider than the dishes. Alternatively, use a large pie dish and roll the dough wider than the dish, as before. Brush the edges of the dishes with beaten egg. Sit the dough on top of the rim and press it over the edge to seal tightly. Brush with more beaten egg, but don't pierce the tops (the steam must be trapped inside). Set the pies on 2 baking sheets and chill for 30 minutes or until ready to bake. Bake at 425°F for 20–25 minutes (or 45 minutes to 1 hour for the large pie) until the dough is risen, crisp, and golden brown. Serve hot.

The perfect cook-and-forget roast. The meat is cooked on a bed of rosemary and onions until it is completely tender all the way through—no pink bits—and the onions are melting into a rosemary gravy. Purée the meat juices with the soft onions for a wonderful, creamy sauce.

pot roast leg of lamb
with rosemary and onion gravy

3 lb. leg of lamb

2 tablespoons olive oil

3 garlic cloves, crushed

2 tablespoons chopped fresh rosemary

3 large rosemary sprigs

2 fresh bay leaves

4 large onions, thinly sliced

1¼ cups dry white wine

2 teaspoons Dijon mustard

sea salt and freshly ground black pepper

Potatoes Dauphinoise (page 101), to serve

Serves 6

Trim the lamb of any excess fat. Heat the oil in a casserole dish in which the lamb will fit snugly. Add the lamb and brown it all over. Remove and let cool.

Crush the garlic and chopped rosemary together with a mortar and pestle. Using a small sharp knife, make small incisions all over the lamb. Push the paste well into these incisions. Season well with salt and pepper.

Put the rosemary sprigs, bay leaves, and onions in the casserole dish and put the lamb on top. Mix the wine with the mustard, then pour into the casserole dish. Bring to a boil, cover tightly, then cook in a preheated oven at 325°F for 1½ hours, turning the lamb over twice.

Raise the oven temperature to 400°F and remove the lid from the casserole dish. Cook for another 30 minutes. The lamb should be very tender and completely cooked through.

Carefully remove the lamb to a serving dish and keep it warm. Skim the fat from the cooking juices and remove the bay leaves and rosemary sprigs. Add a little water if too thick, then bring to a boil, scraping the bottom of the pan to mix in the sediment. Pour the sauce into a blender or food processor and purée until smooth. Taste and season with salt and pepper.

Serve with the lamb with the sauce and potatoes dauphinoise.

This moist and tender cut of pork is basted throughout cooking with the mahogany-colored balsamic vinegar and soy sauce cooking juices that give a wonderful flavor to the meat. Roasting first at a high temperature really helps to concentrate the sauce.

roast loin of pork
with balsamic vinegar

4 lb. boneless pork loin roast, center cut

1–2 tablespoons safflower oil

1¼ cups dry white wine

⅓ cup balsamic vinegar

⅓ cup soy sauce

sea salt and freshly ground black pepper

Serves 6

Check the weight of the meat and calculate the cooking time—you will need 25 minutes for every pound in weight (for 3½ lb., about 1½ hours). Heat the oil in a skillet, add the meat, brown it all over, then transfer to a roasting pan and pour the wine, vinegar, and soy sauce over the pork.

Put the roasting pan on the bottom to middle shelf of a preheated oven at 425°F and cook for 30 minutes.

Baste the pork, then reduce the heat to 375°F, and roast for the remaining calculated time, basting the meat every 20 minutes.

Remove from the oven and let rest in a warm place for 20–30 minutes to set the juices.

Serve the pork thickly sliced with the dark pan juices seasoned with salt and pepper.

Reduced balsamic vinegar To make cheap balsamic vinegar taste rich and delicious, turn it into a concentrated syrup by pouring the whole bottle into a saucepan. Open the kitchen window or turn on the exhaust fan, then boil hard until reduced by half and looking syrupy. Let cool, then pour into a jar and store in the refrigerator. This is wonderful added to stews, soups, and dressings.

vegetarian

This cannelloni can be assembled the day before, refrigerated, and put in the oven at the last moment. You can vary the type of cheese, as long as it is a soft one.

ricotta, basil, and cherry tomato cannelloni

1½ lb. ripe cherry tomatoes, whole, plus 12 oz. vine-ripened tomatoes, thinly sliced (you need 24 slices)

⅓ cup good olive oil

2 teaspoons dried oregano

2 teaspoons sugar

10 oz. ricotta cheese

⅓ cup fresh red or green pesto (page 135)

12 sheets of fresh lasagne

3 tablespoons freshly grated Parmesan cheese

sea salt and freshly ground black pepper

To serve

basil leaves

green salad

a baking dish, 10 x 8 inches, lightly oiled

Serves 4

Cut 8 oz. of the whole cherry tomatoes in half and set aside for the top.

Heat the oil in a skillet, add the uncut tomatoes (they will splutter a little), and cover tightly. Cook over high heat, shaking the pan occasionally, for 5 minutes until the tomatoes start to break down. Uncover and stir in the oregano, sugar, salt, and pepper. Set aside.

Soften the cheese in a bowl and beat in the pesto. Put all the sheets of lasagne on a work surface and spread the cheese mixture evenly over them. Put 2 tomato slices on each sheet, season well with salt and pepper, and roll up from the narrow side like a jelly roll. Spoon half the tomato sauce in the bottom of the baking dish. Put the pasta rolls on top of the sauce, then spoon over the remaining sauce. Dot with the reserved cherry tomato halves and cover with foil.

Bake in a preheated oven at 425°F for 25–30 minutes. Uncover, sprinkle with the Parmesan, and bake or broil for a further 10 minutes until beginning to brown. Remove from the oven and let stand for 10 minutes before serving.

Top with the basil and serve with a crisp green salad.

Note If using dried lasagne sheets, cook in boiling salted water according to the package instructions. Carefully lift them out of the water and drain in a colander. Transfer to a bowl of cold water. Lift out and drain each sheet before spreading with the cheese mixture.

The bigger and darker the mushrooms, the better their flavor. Laced with garlic and a hint of rosemary, they are sublime. Creamy fresh goat cheese cuts the richness of the filling. I used walnuts, but any nuts will do.

mushroom, walnut, and goat cheese tart

1 recipe Short-Crust Pastry Dough (see note)

6 tablespoons unsalted butter

1 onion, thinly sliced

2 garlic cloves, finely chopped

1 tablespoon chopped fresh rosemary

1 lb. large, dark portobello mushrooms, sliced

finely grated zest and juice of 1 unwaxed lemon

3 large eggs, beaten

8 oz. mild goat cheese, softened

1 cup walnuts, coarsely chopped

sea salt and freshly ground black pepper

tomato and arugula salad, to serve

a deep fluted tart pan, 10 inches diameter

parchment paper and baking beans

Serves 6

Put the dough on a floured work surface, roll out thinly, and use to line the tart pan. Prick the base, then cover with parchment paper and baking beans. Bake in a preheated oven at 400°F for 10–12 minutes, remove from the oven, remove the paper and beans, and return to the oven to cook for another 5–7 minutes. The tart crust can be made in advance.

When ready to cook the tart, keep the oven heat at 400°F. Melt the butter in a skillet, add the onion, then the garlic, and sauté for 10 minutes until soft and golden. Stir in the rosemary. Add the mushrooms, lemon zest and juice, salt, and pepper and sauté over medium heat for 5 minutes until the mushrooms are tender and the liquid has evaporated. Let cool slightly.

Put the eggs and half the goat cheese in a bowl, beat well, then stir into the mushroom mixture. Season well. Pour into the baked tart crust and spread evenly. Slice the remaining goat cheese thinly and dot all over the surface. Sprinkle with the chopped walnuts and bake in the preheated oven for 20–25 minutes until set and golden on top. Serve warm with tomato and arugula salad.

Note Short-Crust Pastry Dough

Sift 1⅔ cups all-purpose flour and a pinch of salt into a food processor. Add 1 stick unsalted butter (chilled and chopped) and blend for 30 seconds until the mixture looks like bread crumbs. Add 2–3 tablespoons chilled water and process for 10 seconds to bring the dough together. If necessary, add another tablespoon of water and repeat. Transfer to a floured work surface, knead lightly, then shape into a flattened ball, wrap in plastic wrap, and chill for at least 30 minutes before rolling out.

Good felafel are light and full of flavor. It really is worth using dried and soaked chickpeas—canned ones will make the mix too soft. The felafel should be bright green with herbs, and are a wonderful snack to serve with drinks, as well as making an ideal protein-rich entrée or a light lunch for vegetarian guests.

felafel with avocado, tomato, and red onion salsa

1¼ cups dried chickpeas, soaked in cold water for 24 hours

2 garlic cloves, crushed

1 teaspoon ground cumin

½ teaspoon ground coriander

a pinch of chili powder (optional)

½ teaspoon baking soda

2 scallions, very finely chopped

3 tablespoons chopped fresh flat-leaf parsley

3 tablespoons chopped fresh cilantro

sea salt and freshly ground black pepper

safflower oil, for deep-frying

pita bread, to serve

Avocado, tomato, and red onion salsa

4 ripe tomatoes

1 large ripe avocado

½ red onion, finely chopped

½ small fresh red chile, halved, seeded, and very finely chopped

3 tablespoons chopped fresh cilantro

finely grated zest and juice of 1 unwaxed lime

2–3 tablespoons olive oil

sea salt and freshly ground black pepper

a tray lined with plastic wrap

an electric deep-fryer (optional)

Serves 4

Start the day before. Soak the chickpeas in plenty of cold water. The next day, drain them very well and roll in paper towels to dry them. Transfer to a food processor, add the garlic, cumin, coriander, chili powder, and baking soda, and blend to a smooth paste. Taste and season well with salt and pepper. Tip into a bowl, cover, and let rest for 30 minutes.

Add the scallions, parsley, and cilantro to the chickpea paste, beat thoroughly, then knead the mixture well to bring it together. Line a tray with plastic wrap. Scoop out small lumps and make into flat, round cakes—as small or large as you like—and put them on the tray. Cover and chill for 15 minutes.

Meanwhile, to make the salsa, cut the tomatoes in half, seed them, then chop finely and put in a bowl. Chop the avocado and add to the bowl. Add the onion, chile, and cilantro and stir gently. Put the lime juice, zest, olive oil, salt, and pepper in a small bowl and mix well. Pour over the tomato mixture, fold gently, and set aside.

Fill a saucepan or deep-fryer one-third full with the oil, or to the manufacturer's recommended level. Heat to 355°F or until a cube of bread browns in 30 seconds. Cook, in batches if necessary, for 2–3 minutes until they are crisp and brown, turning them over once. Lift out with a slotted spoon and drain on paper towels. Serve hot or warm, with pita bread and the salsa.

You couldn't find a simpler pasta dish to prepare. It makes a very elegant appetizer when served in small portions, or a filling entrée. Try to keep the butter melted for as long as possible so the lemon oil is fully infused.

tagliolini with lemon and green olives

2 unwaxed lemons

1 stick unsalted butter

¾ cup green olives, pitted and chopped

1 tablespoon chopped fresh lemon thyme (optional)

8 oz. pasta such as egg tagliolini, paglia e fieno, or linguine

½ cup grated Parmesan or pecorino cheese, plus extra to serve

sea salt and freshly ground black pepper

Serves 4 as an appetizer: 2 as an entrée

Grate the zest from the lemons, making sure you grate only the yellow zest and not the bitter white pith.

Melt the butter slowly in a stainless steel or non-reactive pan and add the grated zest. Leave over a very gentle heat or in a warm place to infuse for at least 2 hours (or for as long as you have), remelting if necessary.

When ready to eat, strain the melted butter (reheating if necessary), then add the chopped olives, lemon thyme, if using, and salt and pepper to taste. Keep it warm.

Cook the pasta in a large saucepan of boiling salted water, according to the package instructions. Drain, reserving 2–3 tablespoons of the cooking water. Toss the pasta with the lemon and olive butter, cheese, more pepper if you like, and some of the reserved cooking water if it looks too dry. Serve immediately with extra cheese.

Variations
• Add lots of cracked black pepper to the strained lemon butter. Omit the olives and add 2¼ cups chopped arugula and plenty of grated Parmesan.
• Instead of the lemon zest, infuse bay leaves in the butter and add 8 oz. halved cherry tomatoes.

3 tablespoons olive oil

3 lb. mild onions, finely sliced

3 garlic cloves, chopped

1 teaspoon dried herbes de Provence

Tomato sauce

2 tablespoons olive oil

28 oz. (4 cups) canned chopped tomatoes

3 tablespoons strained tomatoes

1 tablespoon capers, rinsed and drained

1 teaspoon Harissa Sauce (page136), (optional)

⅔ cup dry white wine

sea salt and freshly ground black pepper

Yeast dough

1 cake compressed yeast, 1 teaspoon fast-action dried yeast, or 2 teaspoons regular dried yeast

a pinch of sugar

1 cup all-purpose flour, plus extra for rolling

4 tablespoons unsalted butter, chilled and chopped

1 large egg, beaten

a pinch of sea salt

To finish

red bell pepper strips or about 10 anchovy fillets (optional)

extra olive oil, for drizzling

12–18 small black olives

a jelly-roll pan, 13 x 8 inches

Serves 4–6

This is my favorite summer picnic food—the taste of the seaside in the South of France. Soft, sweet onions scented with Provençal herbs are spread over a layer of concentrated sunshine (tomato sauce), then topped with red bell pepper strips or salty anchovies and black olives, all on a thin, yeasty base. Cut into squares and wrap in foil to take on a picnic.

pissaladière

Heat the oil in a large saucepan, add the onions and garlic, and stir well to coat with the oil. Add 1–2 tablespoons water, cover tightly, and simmer over very low heat for about 1 hour until meltingly soft. Stir from time to time to prevent them sticking, but don't let them color. Add a little more water if they look dry. Stir in the herbs. Drain the mixture into a strainer over a bowl and reserve the liquid for the yeast dough.

To make the tomato sauce, heat the oil in a saucepan, add the olive oil, tomatoes, tomato purée, capers, harissa sauce, if using, white wine, salt, and pepper. Mix well and bring to a boil. Simmer, uncovered, for about 1 hour, stirring occasionally, until well reduced and very thick. Taste and add a little salt and pepper if necessary. Set aside.

To make the yeast dough, cream the compressed yeast in a bowl with the sugar, then whisk in 3 tablespoons of the warmed reserved onion liquid. Leave for 10 minutes until frothy. For other yeasts, use according to the package instructions. Sift the flour into a bowl and rub in the butter. Make a hollow in the center, add the egg, yeast mixture, and a pinch of salt, and mix to a very soft dough—add more onion liquid if it seems dry. Knead in the bowl for 1–2 minutes until smooth. Put in an oiled bowl, cover with plastic wrap, and let rise for 1 hour or until doubled in size.

Punch down the dough, knead lightly, then roll out on a lightly floured surface. Use to line the pan, pushing the dough well up the edges. Spread the reduced tomato sauce thinly over the dough base. Cover with the onions. Arrange the bell pepper strips, if using, in a lattice on top of the onions. Alternatively, cut the anchovies in half lengthwise and use them instead. Drizzle with a little olive oil and bake in a preheated oven at 375°F for about 1 hour until the top is golden and crisp. Arrange the olives on top and serve warm or cold.

Not only is this completely vegetarian, but carnivores love it too. It is delicious, rich, and substantial enough to serve on a cold winter's night. Sometimes, I cook some thinly sliced onions to a crisp caramel and scatter these on top. Mint tea (page 132) is delicious to drink after this dish.

sesame and mint couscous
with winter vegetables

2 tablespoons unsalted butter

2 garlic cloves, finely crushed

1 tablespoon sweet paprika

2 teaspoons ground cumin

½ teaspoon ground ginger

1 teaspoon sea salt

1 teaspoon freshly ground black pepper

2 bay leaves

2 tablespoons strained tomatoes

14 oz. (2 cups) canned chopped tomatoes

2 whole fresh green chiles

2 thick carrots, peeled, quartered, and cut into finger lengths

2 thick parsnips, peeled, quartered, and cut into finger lengths

1 lb. potatoes, peeled and cut into 2-inch chunks

2 thick zucchini, quartered and cut into finger lengths

8 oz. butternut squash or pumpkin, peeled, seeded, and cut into 2-inch chunks

2 tablespoons harissa sauce mixed with ½ cup hot water, to serve

Sesame and mint couscous

2 cups instant couscous

1 stick butter, cut into pieces

¼ cup chopped fresh mint

3 tablespoons toasted sesame seeds

sea salt and freshly ground black pepper

Serves 6

Melt the butter in a heavy casserole dish, add the garlic, and cook for 1 minute over medium heat. Add the paprika, cumin, ginger, salt, pepper, bay leaves, strained tomatoes, and canned tomatoes and stir well. Bring to a boil and add the chiles, carrots, and parsnips.

Pour in enough water to cover (about 1¾ cups), bring to a boil, partially cover with a lid, then simmer gently for 20 minutes. Add the potatoes, zucchini, and butternut squash, pushing them under the liquid, and cook for a further 20 minutes or until the potatoes are tender. Do not overcook or the vegetables will disintegrate.

Meanwhile, put the couscous in a bowl. Put 2 cups boiling water in a heatproof measuring cup, stir in the butter and mint, then pour evenly over the couscous. Cover tightly with plastic wrap and let stand for 5 minutes.

Uncover the couscous and fluff up the grains with a fork. Stir in the sesame seeds, taste, and season well with salt and pepper. Pile the couscous onto a large serving platter, make a hollow in the center, and heap the spicy vegetable stew into the middle. Serve immediately with the harissa sauce mixture in a small bowl.

Note Harissa sauce is widely available in larger supermarkets, gourmet stores, and Middle Eastern stores. To make your own, see the recipe on page 136.

This pretty gratin is bursting with all the flavors of the sun and is based on the tian, a Provençal classic. You can vary the vegetables according to whatever you have available. It's good with zucchini, peppers, potatoes, or onions—and there are even non-vegetarian versions that include boneless chicken pieces. This makes a wonderful dish to serve on its own with a green salad and plenty of focaccia.

tomato and eggplant gratin
with tomato and chile pesto

2 medium eggplant

about ⅔ cup olive oil

1 lb. ripe red tomatoes

1 quantity Tomato and Chile Pesto (page 135)

¼ cup chopped fresh basil

1¼ cups freshly grated Parmesan cheese

sea salt and freshly ground black pepper

a shallow ovenproof dish, buttered

Serves 4

Using a sharp knife, cut the eggplant into ¼-inch slices. Sprinkle with salt and put in a colander to drain for 30 minutes. Rinse well and pat dry with paper towels.

Brush the eggplant with olive oil and cook under a preheated broiler on both sides until brown. Drain on paper towels.

Cut the tomatoes in half through the middle.

Arrange a layer of eggplant in the dish, followed by a few spoonfuls of pesto, followed by layer of tomatoes. Sprinkle with the basil, then the Parmesan. Season with salt and pepper, then repeat, finishing with a layer of eggplant. Sprinkle the remaining Parmesan over the top.

Bake in a preheated oven at 400°F for 25–30 minutes until browned and bubbling on top. Cool slightly, then serve warm, or let cool completely and serve chilled as a salad.

vegetables
and salads

This Caesar isn't Roman—it was invented in 1924 by restaurateur Caesar Cardini, "south of the border, down Mexico way." In fact, the only thing Roman about it is the kind of lettuce used—romaine.

caesar salad

1 romaine lettuce

⅔ cup olive oil

2 large garlic cloves, crushed

2 tablespoons freshly squeezed lemon juice, from about 1 medium lemon

½ teaspoon Dijon mustard

2 anchovy fillets in oil, drained

1 large egg yolk

2 slices of stale bread, crusts removed, cubed

2 tablespoons freshly grated Parmesan cheese

sea salt and freshly ground black pepper

Serves 4

Pull the leaves off the lettuce, wash them, and tear into bite-size pieces. Spin in a salad spinner or dry on paper towels. Store in a sealed plastic bag in the refrigerator to keep it crisp.

Put 3 tablespoons olive oil in a blender or food processor and add half the garlic, the lemon juice, mustard, anchovies, and egg yolk. Blend until smooth, then transfer to a pitcher, taste, and season with salt and pepper.

Pour the remaining olive oil into a skillet and heat until the garlic starts to sizzle. Scoop out the garlic, then add the cubed bread. Sauté until golden, keeping the pieces on the move while they are cooking. Lift out and drain on paper towels.

Stir the dressing, pour over the salad leaves, toss well, then transfer to a bowl. Add the croutons and sprinkle with the Parmesan. Serve immediately.

If anchovies don't appeal, liven up the dressing with a dash of Worcestershire sauce. You can use other kinds of salad leaves, such as radicchio, iceberg, or Chinese leaves—just remember that they must be crisp to bring out the crunchiness of the salad.

Always make dressings fresh Whisk the ingredients in the bottom of the salad bowl, then add the leaves and toss well to coat.

This is a great prepare-ahead dish for a crowd. You can use any type of Asian noodle for this; there are so many available today—some dried, some ready-to-use. Even Italian pasta works well with this peanut sauce.

cold noodles
with peanut sauce

1 lb. noodles

1 tablespoon sesame oil or safflower oil

1 teaspoon Szechuan peppercorns

1 inch fresh ginger, peeled and coarsely chopped

2 large juicy garlic cloves

¼ cup smooth peanut butter

¼ cup soy sauce

3 teaspoons chile oil (chile-flavored oil)

½ teaspoon salt

2 teaspoons sugar

6 scallions, finely sliced diagonally

3 tablespoons raw peanuts, toasted and coarsely chopped

Serves 4

Cook the noodles according to the package instructions, depending on type. Drain, rinse well, and let drain for a couple of minutes. Add a little sesame oil and toss gently.

Heat a small skillet and toast the Szechuan peppercorns for a couple of minutes until they smell aromatic and begin to smoke a little. Do not let them burn. Tip into a bowl and let cool. Grind to a powder using a pepper grinder or mortar and pestle.

Transfer to a food processor, add the ginger, garlic, peanut butter, soy sauce, chile oil, salt, sugar, and ½ cup warm water and process until smooth and creamy. Beat in extra warm water if too thick. Add the sauce to the noodles, toss well, then transfer to a serving dish and sprinkle the scallions and peanuts on top.

Szechuan peppercorns, sometimes known as Chinese pepper or fagara, are little brown berries that are dried and roasted to bring out their spicy, woody flavor. They are readily available in larger supermarkets. If you can't find them, use black pepper and a tiny pinch of Chinese five-spice powder.

ratatouille

One of those reliable recipes that just gets better as it matures, ratatouille can be served with many dishes, and also by itself with lots of crusty bread. Don't use green bell peppers—they are too bitter.

2 eggplant

3 bell peppers (red, yellow, or orange)

3 tablespoons olive oil

2 large onions, thinly sliced

2 garlic cloves, crushed

2 teaspoons finely crushed coriander seeds

⅓ cup white wine

14 oz. (2 cups) canned chopped tomatoes

1 teaspoon sugar

about 20 dry-cured kalamata olives

sea salt and freshly ground black pepper

parsley leaves, to serve (optional)

Serves 6

Cut the eggplant into large, bite-size pieces, put them in a colander, sprinkle well with salt, and let drain for 1 hour. Cut the peppers in half, remove the white membrane and seeds, and slice the flesh into thick strips.

Heat the olive oil in a heatproof casserole dish and sauté the onions, crushed garlic, and coriander seeds until soft and transparent, but not colored. Add the wine and boil to reduce.

Meanwhile, rinse and drain the eggplant and dry on paper towels. Add the peppers and eggplant to the casserole dish and cook for about 10 minutes, stirring occasionally until softening around the edges, but not browning. Add the tomatoes, sugar, and olives. Heat to simmering point, season well with salt and pepper, then partially cover with a lid and cook for about 25 minutes. Sprinkle with parsley and serve hot or cold.

potatoes dauphinoise

This reheats very well, so is worth making well before the meal to make sure it is perfectly cooked. A good way to start this off is to layer it up in the dish, cover, and microwave it on HIGH for 10 minutes, then finish it off in the oven for 45 minutes.

4 tablespoons unsalted butter, for greasing

2 lb. salad potatoes, thinly sliced

1¼ cups freshly grated Parmesan cheese

freshly grated nutmeg

1¼ cups heavy cream

sea salt and freshly ground black pepper

a shallow ovenproof dish, buttered

Serves 6

Layer the potatoes in the dish, seasoning each layer with cheese, nutmeg, salt, and pepper. Pour over the cream and sprinkle any remaining cheese over the top. Bake in a preheated oven at 325°F for about 1 hour or until the potatoes are tender and the top is golden and crisp.

green rice

Basmati rice is one of the most flavorful varieties there are, especially when cooked properly. Follow this recipe and you will never have soggy rice again. Green herbs and spinach add an extra dimension.

1½ cups basmati rice

¼ cup coarsely chopped fresh green herbs, such as parsley and cilantro

1 cup frozen chopped spinach, thawed

1 tablespoon safflower oil

Serves 4

Bring a large saucepan of cold salted water to a boil. The size of the pan is crucial—the larger the pan, the more water it holds, therefore the rice moves around as it cooks and doesn't stick. Wash the rice under cold running water until the water runs clear. Drain. Add the rice to the boiling water, return to a rolling boil, and stir once. Boil for exactly 8 minutes, then drain well, return to the pan, stir in the herbs, spinach, and oil, then quickly put on a tight-fitting lid. Let it steam in its own heat for another 10 minutes, then lightly fluff up with a fork. Serve immediately.

perfect mashed potatoes

The secret of perfect mash is the right potato—a floury variety that fluffs up properly. Older potatoes work better than new and you should make sure that they are thoroughly cooked or the mash will be lumpy. The mash will keep warm in a very cool oven (250°F) for up to 2 hours if covered with buttered aluminum foil. Otherwise, cool and reheat gently, beating in extra melted butter and hot milk. If adding herbs, beat in just before serving.

1½ lb. potatoes, such as Yukon Gold, quartered

4 tablespoons unsalted butter

⅓–½ cup milk

sea salt and freshly ground black pepper

Serves 4

Preheat the oven to 300°F. Put the potatoes in a saucepan of salted cold water and bring to a boil. As soon as the water comes to a boil, reduce to a simmer (it's important not to cook the potatoes too quickly), and cook for about 20 minutes. When perfectly cooked, the point of a sharp knife should glide into the center.

Drain in a colander, then set over the hot pan to steam and dry out. Tip the potatoes back into the pan and crush with a fork or potato masher or pass them through a food mill or ricer into the pan. Melt the butter in the milk. Using a wooden spoon, beat the butter and milk into the mash—an electric hand-mixer sometimes helps here. Season with salt and pepper, pile into a warm dish, and serve immediately.

Variation Scallion and Horseradish Mash
Beat in 3 tablespoons chopped scallions sautéed in butter and 2 tablespoons creamed horseradish.

vichy carrots
with fresh ginger

These buttery carrots almost caramelize as they cook, so the ginger adds a spicy punch to cut through the rich sweetness.

2 lb. carrots

2 tablespoons finely chopped fresh ginger

4 tablespoons unsalted butter

½ teaspoon sea salt

2 teaspoons sugar

freshly ground black pepper

3 tablespoons chopped fresh cilantro or parsley

Serves 8

Cut the carrots into thick matchsticks or rounds and put in a saucepan with the ginger, butter, salt, and sugar. Half-cover with water, bring to a boil, and boil steadily, stirring once or twice, until the water has almost disappeared and the carrots are tender.

Reduce the heat and let the carrots brown a little and caramelize. Season with pepper and stir in the cilantro. Serve immediately.

Use big old carrots for Vichy, because they will stand up to longer cooking. If using young carrots, keep them whole and leave some of the green tops on for color.

petits pois à la française

Equally good with fresh or frozen peas, this recipe is great for large numbers. The lettuce adds sweetness to the peas. Perfect with fish or lamb—especially in the spring.

8 oz. (2½ cups) green peas,
fresh or frozen and thawed

1 large Spanish onion, thinly sliced

1 small lettuce, shredded

4 tablespoons unsalted butter

1 teaspoon sugar

2 tablespoons chopped fresh mint

2 tablespoons chopped fresh parsley

sea salt and freshly ground black pepper

Serves 4

Mix the peas, onion, and lettuce together in a casserole dish. Add ⅔ cup water, the butter, sugar, salt, and pepper. Cover tightly and simmer for 30 minutes or bake in the oven at 325°F for 1½ hours until very soft. Stir in the herbs, add salt and pepper to taste, then serve.

roasted mediterranean vegetables

3 small zucchini

1 red bell pepper, quartered and seeded

1 yellow bell pepper, quartered and seeded

2 medium red onions, cut into 8 wedges through the root (keep the roots intact)

1 small eggplant, cut into large cubes

⅓ cup good olive oil

a few drops balsamic vinegar

2 sprigs of fresh thyme

torn basil leaves

Serves 4

Cut the zucchini into halves or fourths. Put the peppers, onions, and eggplant in a large roasting pan. Pour the oil over the vegetables, add a few drops of balsamic vinegar, and toss well. Roast in a preheated oven at 400°F for 35–40 minutes, carefully turning twice, adding the thyme 10 minutes before the vegetables are cooked.

The vegetables should begin to take on color and be tender but not disintegrating. Season them well with salt and pepper and transfer to a serving dish. Strew with the torn basil and serve.

grilled corn
with chile lime butter

Messy and meltingly delicious, grilled corn will be a favorite with a crowd of hungry youngsters. Serve with lots of paper napkins—this is definitely a hands-on dish.

12 ears of corn-on-the-cob, husked

1 stick unsalted butter, melted

a large pinch of chili powder

sea salt and freshly ground black pepper

Chile lime butter

1 teaspoon sweet chile sauce

finely grated zest and juice of 2 unwaxed limes

1 stick unsalted butter, softened

wax paper

Serves 6

To make the butter, beat the chile sauce and lime zest into the butter. Season well, then roll into a cylinder between sheets of damp wax paper. Twist the ends and chill for at least 1 hour until hard.

To grill or broil the corn, melt the butter in a small saucepan and whisk in the chile and lime juice mixture. This will be the basting sauce for the corn.

Preheat an outdoor grill or broiler, add the corn, and cook for at least 10 minutes, basting and turning until golden brown all over, soft, and lightly charred. Slice the chilled butter into disks and serve with the hot grilled corn.

sweet things

This has always been one of my favorite cook-in-advance sweet things. Everybody loves it—adults and children alike. Raspberries are delicious with hazelnut and chocolate, but cherries and strawberries would also work well. Keep the cooled meringue in an airtight box until ready to use. You can make this up to one day ahead.

hazelnut and raspberry pavlova
with hot chocolate sauce

4 extra-large egg whites

a pinch of sea salt

1¼ cups sugar, plus a little extra, to taste

1 teaspoon cornstarch

1 teaspoon pure vanilla extract

1 teaspoon wine vinegar

⅔ cup toasted chopped hazelnuts, plus extra for sprinkling

2 cups heavy cream

8 oz. raspberries, fresh or frozen and thawed

Chocolate sauce and whipped cream

7 oz. bittersweet chocolate

2¾ cups heavy cream

¼ cup sugar, plus 1 tablespoon extra

2 tablespoons unsalted butter

a baking sheet, lined with nonstick parchment paper

Serves 6

Mark the lined baking sheet with a 10-inch circle.

Put the egg whites and salt in a bowl and whisk until very stiff. Gradually whisk in the sugar, one large spoonful at a time, making sure the meringue is really "bouncily" stiff before adding the next spoonful.

Whisk the cornstarch, vanilla, and vinegar into the meringue. Fold in the hazelnuts.

Spoon the meringue into the circle right to the edges, making it as rough as you like, but not too shallow. Make a slight dip in the center.

Bake in a preheated oven at 275°F for about 45 minutes until just beginning to turn the palest brown. Turn off the oven and let cool slowly.

To make the hot chocolate sauce, put the chocolate, 1 cup of the cream, the sugar, and butter in a saucepan. Stir until melted. Pour into a pitcher and keep it warm. Put the remaining cream and the 1 tablespoon sugar in a bowl and whip until soft peaks form.

Carefully peel the parchment paper off the pavlova and set it on a serving dish. Dollop the cream generously on top and sprinkle with the raspberries. Trail the hot chocolate sauce over the top or serve it separately. Serve immediately.

A gloriously delicious tart with fruit nestling in a cooked almond filling. This one is made with cherries, but other fruits are also good—try fresh apricots or plums, halved and pitted, sliced apples, peaches, pears, or no-need-to-soak prunes. Serve with custard, cream, or ice cream.

fruit frangipane tart

1 recipe Rich Short-Crust Pastry Dough (see note)

Frangipane

2 sticks unsalted butter, softened

1 cup sugar

2 large eggs, plus 2 large egg yolks

4 teaspoons kirsch

1¼ cups blanched almonds, very finely ground in a coffee grinder

¼ cup all-purpose flour

1 lb. fresh cherries

⅔ cup warm sieved apricot jam

a tart pan, 11 inches diameter

Serves 6–8

Preheat the oven to 400°F. Preheat a baking sheet. Roll out the dough and use to line an 11-inch tart pan. Prick the base lightly all over with a fork. Freeze until firm.

To make the frangipane, put the butter and sugar in a food processor and beat until light and fluffy. With the machine running, gradually add the whole eggs, egg yolks, and kirsch. Beat in the ground almonds and flour. Spoon the frangipane into the chilled tart crust, spreading it out evenly. Dot with the fruit, pressing down gently until they touch the base. Put on the hot baking sheet for 10–15 minutes until the dough edges begin to brown. Turn the heat down to 350°F and bake for a further 30–35 minutes, until the frangipane is golden brown and set. Transfer to a wire rack to cool. Just before serving, brush the surface with the apricot jam and serve at room temperature.

Note Rich Short-Crust Pastry Dough

Sift 1⅔ cups all-purpose flour and ½ teaspoon salt together into a bowl, then rub in 1 stick plus 1 tablespoon chilled, chopped, unsalted butter. Mix 2 large egg yolks with 2 tablespoons ice water. Add to the flour, mixing together lightly with a knife. (The dough must have some water in it or it will be too difficult to handle. If it is still too dry, add a little more water, sprinkling it over the flour mixture 1 tablespoon at a time.)

Transfer the mixture to a lightly floured work surface. Knead lightly with your hands until smooth, then form into a rough ball. Flatten slightly, then wrap in plastic wrap and chill for at least 30 minutes before rolling out. You can also freeze it, then thaw before rolling out. This recipe makes about 14 oz. dough, enough to line a tart pan 10–11 inches diameter.

Variation For a Sweet Short-Crust Pastry Dough, sift 2 tablespoons confectioners' sugar with the flour and salt.

mixed nut molasses tart

Incredibly rich, this tart can be packed with whatever kinds of nuts you have available. Serve it as a dessert, as here—or in small slices with coffee.

½ recipe Rich Short-Crust Pastry Dough (page 112, note)

⅓ cup molasses

⅓ cup maple syrup

finely grated rind and juice of 1 unwaxed orange

⅔ cup blanched almonds, very finely ground in a coffee grinder

1 cup mixed whole nuts such as walnuts, hazelnuts, pecans, pine nuts, and almonds

custard, cream, or crème fraîche, to serve

a thick baking sheet

a tart pan, 8 inches diameter

Serves 6

Preheat the oven to 375°F and put in the baking sheet.

Roll out the dough to ¼ inch thick. Use to line the tart pan, then trim and prick the base. I like to chill or freeze the dough at this stage. Put the molasses, maple syrup, orange juice, and zest in a saucepan and heat until just warm and runny. Stir in the almonds.

Spread into the frozen tart crust and sprinkle the nuts all over the surface. Transfer to the hot baking sheet in the preheated oven and bake for about 30 minutes or until the filling has just set and the pastry is browning at the edges.

Remove from the oven and let cool slightly before serving warm with real custard, cream, or crème fraîche.

lemon curd tartlets
with blueberry compote

For a super-easy treat to serve with tea or coffee, or as a simple dessert, keep a stack of ready-made tartlet crusts in an airtight container, your own lemon curd (so easy to make) in a jar in the refrigerator, plus a pot of blueberry compote (also wonderful to keep as a breakfast standby).

1 recipe Short-Crust Pastry Dough (page 83, note)

1 recipe Lemon Curd (page 141)

Blueberry compote

1½ cups fresh blueberries

½ cup sugar

3-inch fluted cookie cutter

12-cup bun pan or muffin pan

Make 12 tartlets

Roll out the dough thinly and cut out 12 rounds with the fluted cookie cutter. Use to line a 12-cup pan with the dough, pressing the rounds into the cups. Prick the bases and chill or freeze for 15 minutes. Bake blind without lining with beans, in a preheated oven at 350°F for 5–8 minutes. Remove from the oven and let cool.

To make the compote, put the blueberries in a saucepan with 1 tablespoon water and the sugar. Cook over gentle heat until the sugar dissolves, then bring to a boil and boil for 1 minute. Pour into a bowl to cool, then store in a jar in the refrigerator.

When ready to serve, fill the tartlet cases with a dollop of lemon curd, then spoon blueberry compote on top. Eat immediately.

These little creams have a texture like satin, and a rich coffee flavor. They are so easy to make and turn out very easily; they are a little firmer than usual because they contain mascarpone, a rich creamy cheese.

coffee panna cotta

6 oz. mascarpone cheese

2 cups heavy cream

3 tablespoons ground espresso coffee

⅔ cup sugar

1 vanilla bean, split

¼ cup milk

2 teaspoons powdered gelatin

caramelized walnut halves, to decorate

6 small molds, ½ cup each, lightly oiled

a baking sheet

Serves 6

Put the mascarpone, cream, espresso coffee, sugar, and vanilla bean in a saucepan. Put over low heat until almost but not quite boiling, stirring occasionally. Remove from the heat and leave to infuse for 20 minutes.

Put the milk in another saucepan with the gelatin. Put over very low heat until the gelatin has dissolved. Stir the dissolved gelatin into the hot cream and mascarpone mixture and strain into a measuring cup with a lip.

Pour this hot cream into the lightly oiled molds, let cool, then refrigerate for several hours or overnight until set.

To serve, carefully loosen the creams and invert onto individual plates. Decorate with the walnut halves, then serve at once.

To caramelize walnut halves, melt ½ cup sugar with 3 tablespoons water until completely dissolved. Bring to a boil, then boil rapidly until the sugar starts to smoke and turn a golden caramel color. Quickly stir in 6 walnut halves to coat. Lift each half out with a fork and leave to harden on nonstick parchment paper.

There's so much exotic fruit around in the winter, which is lucky for us because temperate climate varieties disappear at that time. In this recipe, brightly colored fruits are tossed in an unusual fragrant lemongrass and lime syrup, then piled on top of a light yet rich mango mousse. It makes a refreshing end to a big meal or buffet.

mango mousse
with tropical fruit salad

12 oz. ripe mango flesh or 1½ cups purée

1 tablespoon sugar

finely grated zest and juice of 2 unwaxed limes

1 envelope powdered gelatin (1 tablespoon)

⅔ cup heavy cream, lightly whipped

2 large egg whites

Lemongrass syrup

⅔ cup sugar

½ stick of lemongrass, bruised with a rolling pin

finely grated zest and juice of 1 unwaxed lime

Tropical fruit salad

1 very ripe red pomegranate

a selection of fresh exotic fruit, such as papaya, pineapple, yellow melon, lychees, and grapes (you will need about ½ cup prepared fruit per person)

Serves 4

Put the mangoes in a blender or food processor, add the sugar and lime zest and juice, and blend to make a smooth, soft purée. Taste and add more sugar if necessary.

Put 3 tablespoons water in a small saucepan, sprinkle with the gelatin, and leave for 5 minutes to swell and sponge. Let the gelatin dissolve over low heat without boiling until it is liquid and clear, then stir it into the mango purée. Chill for 15 minutes to set slightly, then fold in the lightly whipped cream. Whisk the egg whites until just holding soft peaks and carefully fold into the mango mixture. Spoon into individual glasses, leaving enough room for the fruit salad on top. Chill in the refrigerator for 2–3 hours until set.

Meanwhile, to make the lemongrass syrup, put the sugar in a small, heavy saucepan, add 1¼ cups water, and melt over low heat. When the sugar has completely dissolved, add the lemongrass, increase the heat, and boil for about 2–3 minutes until the syrup feels slippery when tested between the fingers. Remove from the heat, remove the lemongrass, and add the lime juice. Let cool, then stir in the lime zest. Chill.

To prepare the pomegranate, cut in half, then remove the red seeds and reserve them. Discard the skin and pith. To prepare the other fruit, peel, seed, cut into slices or chunks, and put in a bowl. Carefully mix all the fruit together and add the chilled syrup. Mix again to coat, then chill in the refrigerator.

To serve, spoon the fruit salad on top of the set mousses and sprinkle with the pomegranate seeds.

brown sugar meringues

Make these ahead, keep in airtight container, then sandwich together with cream—handy for making last-minute desserts.

4 large egg whites

⅔ cup superfine sugar

⅔ cup firmly packed light brown sugar

a baking sheet lined with nonstick parchment paper

Makes 12

Put the egg whites in a large bowl and whisk until very stiff but not dry. Mix the superfine sugar and brown sugar, then gradually whisk in the combined sugars, spoonful by spoonful, letting the mixture become very stiff between each addition.

Spoon 12 large meringues onto the parchment paper. Bake in a preheated oven at 225°F for 3–4 hours until thoroughly dried out.

Remove the meringues from the oven and let cool on the parchment. Carefully lift off when cool and store in an airtight container until required.

baked bananas
with golden raisin rum ice cream

Adults and kids alike adore baked bananas. This dish takes a Girl Scout campfire recipe to unknown heights of sophistication with golden raisins soaked in rum until plump and juicy. For kids, try soaking the dried fruit in a fruit juice cocktail instead of rum. The raisins can be soaked well beforehand and kept in a jar in the refrigerator.

1¼ cups golden raisins

1¼ cups dark rum

2 pints very good quality real-vanilla ice cream, softened

12 hard butterscotch candies

6 small perfect bananas

Serve 6

Put the raisins and rum in a saucepan, bring to a boil, then cover and let cool and swell for 2–3 hours. Mix half of these into the softened ice cream and replace in the freezer. Reserve the remainder, cover, and chill until needed.

Put the butterscotch candies in a plastic bag and crush with a rolling pin. Cut a strip of skin ½ inch wide lengthwise down the inside curve of each banana, leaving it attached at the stalk end. Scoop out a little of the banana and sprinkle with the crushed butterscotch candies. Bake in a preheated oven at 350°F for 10–15 minutes. Serve the bananas with a scoop of the ice cream and a spoonful of the rum-soaked raisins.

chocolate chile truffles

I like to pass round a mound of these surprisingly warm and mysterious truffles instead of a dessert.

10 oz. bittersweet chocolate

4 tablespoons unsalted butter, cut into pieces

1¼ cups heavy cream

¼ teaspoon hot chili powder

2 tablespoons chile vodka

cocoa powder, for coating

a shallow tray and paper cases

Makes about 20

Put the chocolate, butter, cream, and chili powder in a bowl set over a saucepan of simmering water. Heat until melted—the mixture should be just tepid. Stir occasionally (overmixing will make the mixture grainy). Stir in the vodka.

Pour into a shallow tray and refrigerate until firm. Scoop out teaspoons of mixture, roll into rough balls, and chill. Sift the cocoa powder onto a plate. Carefully roll each truffle in the cocoa. Chill until set. Put in paper cases and store in an airtight container in the refrigerator for up to 2 weeks. They may also be frozen for up to 3 months.

Note Candied Bird's Eye Chiles
These are easy to make and will provide quite a talking point served with the truffles. Remember, they are very hot! Dissolve 1¼ cups sugar in 1¼ cups water in a medium saucepan. Bring to a boil for 1 minute. Drop in 2 oz. whole bird's eye chiles and bring to a boil. Simmer for 15 minutes, then turn off the heat and leave to soak in the syrup for 24 hours. Lift out of the syrup with a fork, drain well, and arrange on nonstick parchment paper. Use immediately while still shiny or roll them in a little extra sugar to coat and let dry at room temperature for 24 hours. Store in layers in an airtight box for up to 1 month.

chinese fortune cookies

These are great fun to make for a surprise ending to a dinner party, for someone's birthday, or just to start the New Year.

⅔ cup all-purpose flour

¼ teaspoon sea salt

2 tablespoons cornstarch

6 tablespoons sugar

2 large egg whites

7 tablespoons olive oil

6 lucky messages written on strips of colored paper

a baking sheet, lightly oiled or lined with nonstick parchment paper

Makes 6

Sift the flour, salt, cornstarch, and sugar together into a bowl. Whisk the egg white in a second bowl with the olive oil and 3 tablespoons water, then beat into the flour until smooth.

Using a tablespoon of batter for each cookie, and cooking no more than 2 at a time, spread out thinly into 7.5 cm rounds on the prepared baking sheet.

Bake in a preheated oven at 350°F for about 5 minutes or until the edges are just browning. Working quickly, lay a paper message across the center of each cookie and fold in half over the paper with the help of a palette knife. Hold the rounded edges of semicircle between thumb and forefinger. Put the forefinger of your other hand at the center of the folded edge and push in, making sure that the solid sides of the cookie puff out. Work quickly because they become brittle as they cool.

Let the cookies cool completely on a wire rack, then store in an airtight container.

drinks

real old-fashioned lemonade

Make this sensational summer drink when lemons are ripe and plentiful. Leave the lemons on a warm windowsill for a few days to sweeten them up and develop their flavor. You can make this a day or two ahead—it MUST be served as cold as possible.

3 unwaxed lemons, scrubbed in warm water

1 cup sugar

1 quart boiling water

sprigs of mint or lemon balm (optional)

Makes about 5 cups

Using a potato peeler, remove the yellow zest from the lemons in long strips, avoiding any bitter white pith. Put it in a large heatproof pitcher, add the sugar, and pour over the boiling water. Stir well to dissolve the sugar, cover, and let cool completely. Squeeze the juice from the lemons, strain, and set aside. When the lemon-scented water is cold, stir in the lemon juice and strain into a pitcher. Chill well and serve poured over ice, perhaps with a sprig of mint or lemon balm.

pear, apple, and kiwifruit juice with fresh ginger

This utterly delicious juice combo is one of my favorite ways to start the day—the ginger adds a surprising warm and lively note. Kiwifruit contains large amounts of vitamin C, and I sometimes add a little watercress or arugula for a green, peppery hit. Juices and smoothies taste much better if the fruit is only just ripe (or even a little underripe); if too ripe, the taste will be dull. Make this recipe in a juicer if you have one, or make into a yogurt smoothie in a blender, in which case it will serve two.

1 not-too-ripe pear

1 apple

2 not-too-ripe kiwifruit

1-inch piece of fresh ginger, peeled and coarsely chopped

Serves 1

Juicer Method Peel and core the pear and the apple and cut into 6 wedges each. Peel the kiwifruit and cut it into fourths. Put the pear through the juicer first, followed by the ginger, kiwifruit, and finally the apple. Stir well before serving, because it can separate. Drink as soon a possible and just feel those vitamins coursing through your body!

Blender Smoothie Put all the prepared fruits and ginger in a blender with ⅔ cup plain yogurt. Blend until smooth, adding a squeeze of lemon juice or a little salt to taste

pussyfoot

Pussyfoot is one of the best non-alcoholic drinks I know, and greatly appreciated by designated drivers and pregnant women. It is grown-up looking and very refreshing, thanks to the mellowing effect of the grenadine (sweet pomegranate syrup). Make sure the juices are freshly squeezed—bottled or carton juice just will not do. Leave out the egg yolk if there's any risk involved—it won't matter greatly and you can always add a tablespoon of cream.

¼ cup freshly squeezed orange juice

2 tablespoons freshly squeezed lemon juice

2 tablespoons freshly squeezed lime juice

1–2 tablespoons grenadine

1 free-range egg yolk (optional)

ice cubes

Makes 1

Pour the orange, lemon and lime juices, grenadine, and optional egg yolk into a cocktail shaker half-filled with ice cubes. Shake well and strain into a glass filled with more ice cubes.

Variation Add a dash of sparkling water or lemonade for fizz.

glögg

This comforting, heart-warming drink is served in cafés in Denmark and Sweden to cheer up bleak winter days. It has a miraculous effect.

2 bottles medium red wine, 750 ml each

⅔ cup sugar

1–1½ cups mixed raisins and slivered almonds

1 cinnamon stick

4 cloves

8 cardamom pods, lightly crushed

1 inch piece of fresh ginger, lightly smashed

¾ cup schnapps or vodka

½ cup brandy or cognac

kitchen twine

Serves 8

Pour 1 bottle of red wine into a non-reactive bowl or saucepan. Add the sugar, raisins, and almonds and stir to dissolve. Put the spices in a cheesecloth bag, tie with kitchen twine, and add to the wine. Leave to infuse for a couple of hours if possible.

Heat the wine until almost boiling, then cover and leave to infuse for at least 30 minutes (you can also do this in the morning if serving it at night). When ready, remove the spice bag and pour in the remaining bottle of wine, the vodka, and brandy. Reheat until almost boiling and serve hot in glass cups with spoons to eat the raisins and almonds.

What would we do for a celebration if champagne had never been invented? A real champagne cocktail can be lethal, so don't plan on serving more than two before a meal—trust me.

champagne cocktails

1 sugar cube
Angostura Bitters
1 teaspoon brandy
cold champagne or sparkling wine

Serves 1

Put a sugar cube in each glass. Add a couple of drops of Bitters, then the brandy and top up with cold champagne.

If the refrigerator is full, buy lots of ice, stand the bottles of wine, water, or juice in a container such as a large cooler, then pack ice all around them. Pour in enough water to immerse the bottles. Put the container in the bath or shower cubicle (hide it behind the shower curtain) and leave for 1 hour—the bottles will be perfectly chilled and there is no need to keep opening and shutting the refrigerator door. For a really large party, fill the whole bath with ice and water and immerse all the bottles. Just pull out the plug after everyone leaves.

I use tangerine, mandarin, or tangelo slices for this sangria, because they add a really exotic touch to the drink, but remember that it's crucial to marinate the base mixture overnight to infuse all the fantastic summery flavors. Make large quantities because people really love it. Sometimes I add Italian limoncello instead of orange liqueur.

white wine sangria

1 bottle dry but full-bodied white wine, 750 ml
2 tablespoons sugar (or to taste)
at least 3 tablespoons orange liqueur
2 small unwaxed oranges, tangerines, or tangelos, sliced
2 unwaxed lemons, sliced
1 cup chilled soda water, sparkling water, or chilled sparkling wine

To serve
apple and peach slices or wedges
sprigs of mint

Makes 1 quart

Put the wine, sugar, liqueur, oranges, and lemons in a large pitcher. Stir, cover, and refrigerate overnight. Strain or not, as you wish, into another pitcher, then add ice and top up with soda water or chilled sparkling wine. Add apple and peach slices and sprigs of mint, then serve.

moroccan mint tea

Mint tea is very soothing after a spicy meal. Don't use spearmint—it will taste like mouthwash.

1½ heaping tablespoons green tea leaves
a handful of whole mint leaves (not spearmint)
about ¾ cup sugar, or to taste

Makes about 1 quart: serves 6

Heat the teapot with just-boiled water. Tip out the water, add the tea leaves, and pour a little boiling water over them just to moisten. Swirl around, then quickly pour the water out again, taking care not to lose any leaves. Add a good handful of fresh mint (the sugar is traditionally added at this stage, but leave it out or serve it later). Pour about 1 quart boiling water over the mint and moistened tea leaves. Put on the lid and leave to infuse for 5–8 minutes. Pour into warmed glasses and top with a few extra mint leaves. Serve the sugar separately.

spiced tea

A deliciously fragrant change from the norm and especially reviving after a long winter's walk, you can make this as strong or as weak as you like. Sometimes I add a teaspoon of condensed milk to each cup—no need for sugar.

1 cinnamon stick
3 cloves
1 whole star anise
3–4 cardamom pods, lightly crushed
1 heaping tablespoon Indian black tea leaves, such as Darjeeling or Assam

Serves 6

Put the cinnamon, cloves, star anise, and cardamom pods in a saucepan, add 1 quart water, and bring to a boil. Reduce the heat, cover, and simmer gently for 5 minutes, then stir in the loose tea. Stir well, cover, and leave to infuse for 5 minutes. Strain into a warmed teapot, and serve as it is, or with sugar and milk.

really good coffee

Proper coffee is very easy to make—and you don't need special pots or hissing machines, just a heatproof pitcher and a fine tea strainer. Hot milk makes all the difference for those who take milk in their coffee; it produces a drink that's almost velvety and keeps it hot, too. Freshly ground coffee is important (freeze the bag after opening, then use straight from frozen). Espresso coffee will take a little longer to settle.

2 tablespoons medium ground coffee per person
boiling water
hot milk

Pour some hot water into a heatproof pitcher to warm it up. Empty out and add the appropriate amount of coffee per person. Pour on enough recently boiled water just to cover the coffee grounds. Stir and leave for 1 minute to infuse.

Top up with 1¼ cups just-boiled water per person and stir well. Cover and let brew for 5 minutes. Either strain through the tea strainer into cups or into another warmed pitcher. Add hot (not boiled) milk, if using. The coffee will have a *crema* or creamy foam on top if you have followed all the steps correctly, and will have a full, rich flavor.

basics and standbys

a selection of pestos

Liven up soups, use to spread on grilled or broiled food or hot toast, stir into a braised dish, or make a dressing for a salad—pestos are so versatile. Once made and stored in a jar, make sure you level the surface each time you use it, then re-cover with olive oil to keep out the air. Pesto freezes well, so when the best basil is around in the summer, I freeze it in ice-cube trays, then keep the cubes in plastic bags. Don't thaw the cubes—just let them melt into whatever's cooking.

walnut and arugula pesto

2 cups arugula leaves

1 garlic clove

½ cup shelled walnuts

3 oz. fresh goat cheese

½ cup olive oil
(or half olive oil, half walnut oil)

freshly ground black pepper

Serves 4

Put all the ingredients in a food processor and blend until smooth, scraping down any bits that cling to the side of the bowl. Spoon into a jar, cover with a thin layer of olive oil to exclude the air, then refrigerate for up to 2 weeks.

basil and lemongrass pesto.

1 garlic clove, peeled

1 stalk of lemongrass, chopped

½ cup macadamia nuts

1½ cups fresh basil leaves (no stalks)

1 tablespoon sesame oil

⅔ cup good olive oil

sea salt and freshly ground black pepper

Serves 4

Put the garlic, lemongrass, and nuts in a food processor and blend until finely ground. Then add the basil, followed by the mixed oils. Spoon into a jar, cover with a thin layer of olive oil to exclude the air, then refrigerate for up to 2 weeks.

tomato and chile pesto

1 large red bell pepper

1½ cups fresh basil leaves (no stalks)

1 garlic clove, crushed

2 tablespoons pine nuts, toasted

2 very ripe tomatoes

6 sun-dried tomatoes in oil, drained

3 tablespoons strained tomatoes

1 teaspoon mild chili powder

½ cup freshly grated Parmesan
or aged pecorino cheese

⅔ cup extra virgin olive oil

Serves 6–8

Broil the bell pepper, turning until blackened all over. Peel off most of the black skin, pull out the stalk, and scrape out the seeds. Put in a food processor with the basil, garlic, pine nuts, tomatoes, sun-dried tomatoes, strained tomatoes, chili powder, and Parmesan and blend until smooth. With the machine running, slowly pour in the olive oil until well blended. Spoon into a jar, cover with a thin layer of olive oil to exclude the air, and refrigerate for up to 2 weeks.

thai curry pastes and harissa sauce

Thai curry pastes and Tunisian harissa sauce are indispensable. Keep them in either the refrigerator or freezer (freeze in ice-cube trays and press out into thick plastic bags—double-wrap them as they are quite pungent). Homemade pastes knock the spots off the bought variety—and you will be in total control of the heat. You can add small amounts to soups and stews, or spread them on fish, meat, and chicken for grilling or broiling.

red thai curry paste

4 large fresh red chiles, halved and seeded

3 shallots or 1 medium onion, peeled

6 garlic cloves

2 tablespoons chopped cilantro stem and root

1 teaspoon finely grated lime zest

½ stalk of lemongrass, coarsely chopped

½ inch fresh ginger, peeled and coarsely chopped

1 teaspoon dried shrimp paste (blachan), anchovy paste, or 3 anchovy fillets

2 teaspoons ground coriander

1 teaspoon ground cumin

1 tablespoon sweet paprika

½ teaspoon freshly ground black pepper

2 tablespoons peanut oil

Makes enough for 6 servings

Put the chiles in a food processor. Add the remaining ingredients and blend until as smooth as possible, scraping down a couple of times. Always sauté the paste for a couple of minutes in a little hot oil before using.

green thai curry paste

4 large fresh green chiles, trimmed

3 shallots or 1 medium onion, peeled

6 garlic cloves

3–4 tablespoons chopped fresh cilantro leaves

1 tablespoon finely grated lime zest and juice of 1 unwaxed lime

½ stalk of lemongrass, coarsely chopped

½ inch fresh ginger, peeled and coarsely chopped

1 teaspoon dried shrimp paste (blachan), anchovy paste, or 3 anchovy fillets

2 teaspoons ground coriander

1 teaspoon ground cumin

½ teaspoon freshly ground black pepper

2 tablespoons peanut oil

Makes enough for 6 servings

Make in exactly the same way as the previous recipe.

For both recipes, if keeping in the refrigerator, spoon into a jar, making sure there are no air pockets, and cover with a layer of oil. Seal and refrigerate for up to 1 month, or freeze as described in the recipe introduction for up to 6 months.

harissa sauce

3 oz. dried mild and hot chiles

1 medium red bell pepper

1 small garlic clove

1 teaspoon coriander seeds

1 teaspoon caraway seeds

1 teaspoon sea salt

3–4 tablespoons olive oil

Makes about 1 cup

Soak the dried chiles in boiling water for 30 minutes. Roast or broil the bell pepper until charred. Rub off the skin and remove the seeds.

Drain the chiles and put in a food processor with the pepper, garlic, the coriander and caraway seeds, salt, and olive oil. Blend until smooth.

Spoon into a jar, packing down carefully to exclude any air pockets. Pour over a thin layer of olive oil to cover the surface, cover, and label.

caramelized onion confit

This confit is the ultimate relish to pile into a grilled steak sandwich and serve with a coarse pâté or a chunk of cheese. I sometimes use black currant jam with a dash or vodka instead of the cassis, and it works very well indeed—sometimes you just have to be creative with what you have.

1 stick unsalted butter

1½ lb. red onions, sliced

½ cup sherry or wine vinegar

¾ cup sugar

3 tablespoons crème de cassis (black currant liqueur)

1¼ cups full-bodied dry red wine

sea salt and freshly ground black pepper

Makes 2 cups

Melt the butter in a skillet, add the onions and vinegar, cover, and simmer for 10 minutes until soft. Add the sugar, increase the heat and cook, stirring, until the onions start to caramelize and the liquid has evaporated. Add the cassis and wine and cook gently, uncovered, for 20 minutes until all the liquid has evaporated. Add salt and pepper to taste, then spoon into a jar, seal, and store in the refrigerator for up to 1 month.

Variation Simple Onion Confit
Melt 4 tablespoons unsalted butter in a skillet and add 2 large sliced onions. Stir to coat with the butter, add 2 tablespoons water, cover, and cook over gentle heat for 10 minutes.

Uncover, sprinkle with 2 teaspoons sugar and 1 tablespoon balsamic vinegar, and increase the heat. Cook over brisk heat for about another 10 minutes, stirring from time to time, but watching it like a hawk. The onions should start to turn a beautiful rich brown color—if not, just cook a little longer. Set aside when cooked.

black olive tapenade

My recipe for this traditional Provençal spread has a more intense, almost smoky flavor.

1 small sweet red bell pepper

3 garlic cloves, unpeeled

1½ cups black olives, preferably dry-cured kalamatas, pitted

2–3 tablespoons salted capers or capers in vinegar, rinsed

12 anchovy fillets in oil or 1 small can tuna in oil, drained

about ⅔ cup olive oil

lemon juice, to taste

freshly ground black pepper

Makes about 2½ cups

Cook the bell pepper and garlic under a hot broiler for about 15 minutes, until completely charred all over (or roast in a hot oven). Let cool, then rub off skin (do not wash) and remove the stalk and seeds. Peel the skin off the garlic. Put the pepper, garlic, olives, capers, and anchovies in a food processor and process until coarsely chopped. With the machine running, slowly add the olive oil until you have a fairly smooth, dark paste. Add lemon juice and pepper to taste. Transfer to a jar, cover with a layer of olive oil to exclude the air, and keep for up to 1 month.

foolproof focaccia

The secret of a truly light focaccia lies in making a very soft dough and letting it rise until really light and puffy.

1 cake compressed yeast, 1 scant tablespoon, or 1 envelope active dry yeast

a pinch of sugar

2 cups warm water

4⅔ cups all-purpose flour

scant ½ cup extra virgin olive oil

coarse sea salt, for sprinkling

2 shallow springform cake pans, 10 inches diameter, lightly oiled

Makes 2 loaves, serves 6–8 each

Cream the fresh yeast and sugar in a bowl, then whisk in the warm water. Leave for 10 minutes until frothy. For other yeasts, use according to the package instructions. Sift the flour into a large bowl and make a hollow in the center. Add the yeast mixture and 3 tablespoons olive oil. Mix until the dough comes together. With clean, dry hands, knead the dough on a lightly floured surface for 5 minutes until smooth, elastic, and quite soft. If too soft to handle, knead in a little more flour, but not much— it should be very soft.

Divide the dough in half, shape each piece into a ball, then roll out to 10-inch rounds. Put in the oiled pans, cover with a clean damp cloth or oiled plastic wrap, and let rise in a warm place for 30 minutes or until very light and puffed up.

Uncover and, using your fingertips, make deep dimples all over the surface of the dough down to the base. Drizzle with the remaining oil. Cover again and let rise once more (30 minutes in a warm place), until doubled in size and very light and puffy. Sprinkle generously with salt. Spray with water and bake in a preheated oven at 400°F for 20–25 minutes until golden brown. Spray with water twice during cooking if you can. Transfer to a wire rack to cool. Eat the same day or freeze as soon as it is cool.

oatmeal sodabread

There's no yeast in this bread, so the quicker you make it and get it in the oven, the better it will be. After baking, store in a plastic bag or airtight container to keep moist. Sodabread is always best eaten warm. Play around with all sorts of additions: cooked chopped bacon and sage, sun-dried tomatoes and olives, poppyseeds, safflower and pumpkin seeds— the list is endless. Bake in a pan or straight on a baking sheet. It freezes very well for up to a month.

about ¾ cup milk, plus extra for glazing

2 tablespoons lemon juice

1½ cups whole-wheat flour

¾ cup all-purpose flour

¾ cup rolled oats

1½ teaspoons baking soda

1½ teaspoons cream of tartar

¾ teaspoon sea salt

3 tablespoons unsalted butter

a deep cake pan, 7 inches diameter, lightly brushed with oil

Makes 1 round loaf, 7 inches diameter

Mix the milk with the lemon juice and leave for 5 minutes. Put the two flours, oats, baking soda, cream of tartar, and salt in a large bowl. Mix well, then rub in the butter. Stir the milk into the dry ingredients to form a soft, slightly sticky dough, adding a little extra milk if necessary. Knead very lightly and quickly (this is the secret to a light, crumbly sodabread) until just smooth. Pat out the dough lightly and use to fill the prepared pan. Brush the top with a little milk. Bake in a preheated oven at 425°F for about 30 minutes or until the base sounds hollow when given a sharp tap. Do not overcook or the bread will become very dry.

prunes or cherries in armagnac or brandy

Make a huge jar of these to store in the refrigerator. They can be served as they are after a meal or with a scoop of cream or ice cream. They are also good baked into a custard tart or cheesecake and are utterly fab chopped up and stirred into softened chocolate ice cream, then frozen for later.

12 oz. large sweet pitted prunes or pitted fresh cherries

⅔ cup Armagnac or brandy

¾ cup sweet white wine

1 vanilla bean, split

½ cup sugar

a strip of unwaxed lemon zest

1 cinnamon stick

Serves 4

Soak the prunes overnight in the Armagnac and wine. Lift out the fruit with a slotted spoon and drop into a preserving jar. Pour the wine into a saucepan and add the vanilla bean, sugar, lemon zest, and cinnamon. Bring to a boil then pour over the prunes. Seal immediately, cool, and store in the refrigerator for up to 3 months.

a pot of jam

I recently discovered this wonderful way of making small quantities of jam in the microwave.

1 lb. fresh ripe strawberries, hulled and quartered

1¾ cups sugar with added pectin (sometimes known as "jam sugar"—see right)

Makes 1½ pots, 1 lb. each

Put the strawberries in a large bowl with a splash of water. Cover and microwave on FULL for 2 minutes. Carefully uncover and stir in the sugar. Re-cover and cook on FULL for another 2 minutes.

Uncover and stir well to dissolve the sugar. Replace in the microwave uncovered and cook on FULL for 8 minutes.

Test by dropping a teaspoon onto a chilled saucer and chilling in the refrigerator for 10 minutes. If it has set up, pour the jam into clean dry jars and cover. If not, microwave for 4 more minutes, then try the test again. Pour into warm, sterilized jars and seal. After opening, the jam will keep in the refrigerator for up to 2 weeks.

To sterilize jam jars, wash them in hot, soapy water and rinse in boiling water. Place in a large saucepan and cover with hot water. With the lid on, bring the water to a boil and continue boiling for 15 minutes. Turn off the heat, then leave the jars in the hot water until just before they are to be filled. Invert the jars onto a clean cloth to dry. Sterilize the lids for 5 minutes, by boiling, or according to the manufacturer's instructions. The jars should be filled and sealed while they are still hot.

lemon curd

6 large eggs

3 large unwaxed lemons

1 stick plus 2 tablespoons unsalted butter

2½ cups sugar

Makes about 1 quart

Separate 2 of the eggs (freeze the whites for use at a later date in meringues). Beat the 2 egg yolks with the remaining 4 whole eggs until completely blended.

Finely grate the zest from all the lemons, but squeeze the juice from only 2.

Melt the butter in a bowl set over a saucepan of simmering water, then stir in the sugar. When warm, pour the beaten eggs through a strainer into the saucepan, then add the lemon juice and zest. Cook, stirring all the time for about 20 minutes or until the curd has thickened considerably. If you are brave enough, you can cook this over direct heat, watching that it doesn't get too hot and separate. Strain into warm, dry, sterilized jars and seal.

Store in the refrigerator for no longer than 3 months absolute maximum.

uncooked freezer raspberry jam

There is no boiling needed for this recipe, so you keep the taste of fresh raspberries. Commercially produced "jam sugar" is perfect for this—it has added pectin that helps the jam thicken to a soft set. Use ½ cup liquid pectin, if you can't find this special jam sugar.

1½ lb. fresh raspberries

5 cups sugar with added pectin (sometimes known as "jam sugar")

2 tablespoons freshly squeezed lemon juice

Makes 2 pots, 16 oz. each

Tip the raspberries into a bowl and mash a bit with a potato masher. Stir in the jam sugar and lemon juice. Cover with plastic wrap and heat on MEDIUM in the microwave for about 5 minutes or until warmed through.

Uncover and stir gently to dissolve the sugar, then leave to stand overnight. Alternatively, heat in a saucepan until the sugar has dissolved.

The next day, pot up into freezer containers and freeze—keep one pot in the refrigerator for breakfast tomorrow. After removing from the freezer, store the jam in the refrigerator. Thaw before using.

menu planner

Vegetarian Lunch
- Mushroom, Walnut, and Goat Cheese Tart OR
- Ricotta, Basil, and Cherry Tomato Cannelloni
- Caesar Salad
- Really Good Coffee
- Chocolate Chile Truffles

Summer
- Jellied Bloody Marys with Tapenade Toasts
- Whole Poached Salmon with Sweet and Sour Pickled Cucumber
- Green Rice (hot or cold)
- Hazelnut and Raspberry Pavlova with Hot Chocolate Sauce

Summer in the Garden
- White Sangria
- Jeweled Gazpacho
- Salmon Steaks with Hot Pesto and Tomatoes
- Brown Sugar Meringues OR
- Coffee Panna Cotta

Barbecue Party
- Guacamole and Tortilla Chips
- Moroccan Butterflied Lamb
- Roasted Mediterranean Vegetables
- Grilled Corn with Chile Lime Butter
- Bananas with Golden Raisin Rum Ice Cream

Italian Flavors
- Grilled Goat Cheese and Rosemary Bruschetta with Baked Garlic Cloves OR
- Tagliolini with Lemon and Green Olives
- Tuscan Chicken
- Perfect Parmesan Mash
- Roasted Mediterranean Vegetables
- Coffee Panna Cotta

Picnic
- Fiery Red Bell Pepper Soup (in a thermos if it's a cold day)
- Real Old-Fashioned Lemonade
- Pissaladière
- Tuscan Chicken (cold)
- Mushroom, Walnut, and Goat Cheese Tart
- Fillet of Beef Salad with Thai Dressing
- Cold Noodles with Peanut Sauce
- Lemon Curd Tartlets (fill on site)

Cold Buffet
- Jellied Bloody Marys with Tapenade Toasts
- Baba Ghanoush
- Whole Poached Salmon with Sweet and Sour Pickled Cucumber
- Fillet of Beef Salad with Thai Dressing
- Cold Noodles with Peanut Sauce
- Green Rice (hot or cold)
- Hazelnut and Raspberry Pavlova with Hot Chocolate Sauce
- Fruit Frangipane Tart
- Mango Mousse with Tropical Fruit Salad

Hot Buffet
- A Big Pot of Cassoulet
- Ricotta, Basil, and Cherry Tomato Cannelloni
- Tomato and Eggplant Gratin
- Caesar Salad
- Hazelnut and Raspberry Pavlova with Hot Chocolate Sauce

A Crowd of Teenagers
- Oven-Roasted Spiced Nuts
- Guacamole and Tortilla Chips
- Baba Ghanoush
- Mexican Pork and Beans
- Prawn Green Curry with Noodles (or with tofu for vegetarians)
- Green Rice
- Mango Mousse with Tropical Fruit Salad OR
- Hazelnut and Raspberry Pavlova with Hot Chocolate Sauce
OR
- Tapenade Toasts
- Moules Marinières Feast
- Mango Mousse with Tropical Fruit Salad

Kids are Coming
- Leek and Potato Soup (with Watercress Purée for the adults)
- Perfect Roast Fillet of Beef with Herbed Yorkshire Puddings
- Perfect Mashed Potatoes
- Vichy Carrots
- Petits Pois à la Française
or
- A Big Pot of Cassoulet
- Coffee Panna Cotta OR
- Lemon Curd Tartlets

Taste of the Middle East
- Dukka
- Felafel
- Baba Ghanoush
OR
- Chickpea Chermoula Soup
- Moroccan Butterflied Lamb
- Sesame and Mint Couscous with Winter Vegetables
- Fruit Frangipane Tart
- Moroccan Mint Tea

Asian Angles
- Smoked Salmon and Cucumber Sushi Rolls
- Prawn Green Curry with Noodles (or with tofu for vegetarians)
- Fillet of Beef Salad with Thai Dressing
- Cold Noodles with Peanut Sauce
- Mango Mousse with Tropical Fruit Salad
- Chinese Fortune Cookies

Winter Feast
- Chicken Liver Parfait with Bitter Orange and Onion Chutney
- Perfect Roast Beef with Herbed Yorkshire Puddings
- Perfect Mashed Potatoes
- Vichy Carrots
- Petits Pois à la Française
- Mixed Nut Molasses Tart OR
- Chocolate Chile Truffles

Cosy Comforting Supper
- Leek and Potato Soup with Watercress Purée
- Pot Roast Leg of Lamb with Garlic Sauce OR
- Steak and Wild Mushroom Pies
- Dauphinoise Potatoes
- Tomato and Eggplant Gratin with Tomato and Chile Pesto
- Bananas with Golden Raisin Rum Ice Cream

Late-Night Supper
- Parmesan and Rosemary Palmiers
- Moules Marinières (have it all ready to cook at the last minute)
OR
- Ricotta, Basil, and Cherry Tomato Cannelloni
- Coffee Panna Cotta
- Chocolate Chile Truffles

index

a

anchovies: black olive tapenade, 137
  Caesar salad, 97
  pissaladière, 88
  tapenade toast, 46
Armagnac, prunes or cherries in, 139
avocados: the best guacamole, 14
  felafel with avocado, tomato, and
    red onion salsa, 84

b

baba ghanoush, 50
bacon: bacon and eggs in a pan, 36
  sausage and bacon rolls, 39
  see also pancetta
balsamic vinegar: reducing, 76
  roast loin of pork with, 76
bananas with raisin rum ice cream,
    120
beans: a big pot of cassoulet, 26
  Mexican pork and beans, 29
beef: fillet of beef salad, 22
  perfect roast fillet of beef, 71
  steak and wild mushroom pies, 72
bell peppers: fiery red bell pepper
    soup, 56
  jeweled gazpacho, 54
  tomato and chile pesto, 135
blueberry compote, lemon curd
    tartlets with, 115
bread: broiled goat cheese and
    rosemary
  Caesar salad, 97
  foolproof focaccia, 138
  bruschetta, 49
  oatmeal sodabread, 138
  see also toast
brown sugar meringues, 120
bruschetta, broiled goat cheese and
    rosemary, 49
butter, chile lime, 106

c

Caesar salad, 97
candied birds' eye chiles, 123
cannelloni, ricotta, basil, and cherry
    tomato, 80
caramelized onion confit, 137
caramelizing walnut halves, 116
carrots, Vichy, 105
cassoulet, 26
champagne cocktails, 131
cheese: Caesar salad, 97
  olive oil and Parmesan mash, 68
  Parmesan and rosemary palmiers,
    13

ricotta, basil, and cherry tomato
    cannelloni, 80
  tomato and eggplant gratin with
    pesto, 92
  see also goat cheese
cherries: cherries in Armagnac or
    brandy, 139
  fruit frangipane tart, 112
chicken: chicken with forty cloves of
    garlic, 67
  chicken with Tuscan herbs, 68
  a fabulous paella, 21
  chicken liver parfait, 53
chickpeas: chickpea chermoula
    soup, 56
  felafel, 84
chile lime butter, 106
chile vodka: chocolate chile truffles,
    123
chiles: candied birds' eye chiles, 123
  fiery red bell pepper soup, 56
  Mexican pork and beans in red
    chile sauce, 29
  sesame and mint couscous with
    winter vegetables, 91
  tomato and chile pesto, 135
Chinese fortune cookies, 123
chocolate: chocolate chile truffles, 123
  hazelnut and raspberry pavlova
    with hot chocolate sauce, 111
chutney, bitter orange and onion, 53
coffee: coffee panna cotta, 116
  really good coffee, 132
cookies: Chinese fortune cookies, 123
  Parmesan and rosemary palmiers,
    13
corn, grilled, 106
court bouillon, 18
couscous, sesame and mint, 91
cucumber: smoked salmon and
    cucumber sushi rolls, 45
  whole poached salmon with
    sweet and sour pickled
    cucumber, 18
curry: green shrimp curry, 60
  Thai curry pastes, 136

d

dips, 14, 50
dressings, Thai, 22
drinks, 124–35
dukkah, 17

e

eggplant: baba ghanoush, 50
  tomato and eggplant gratin, 92

eggs: bacon and eggs in a pan, 36
  fearless scrambled eggs, 36

f

felafel, 84
focaccia, foolproof, 138
fruit: fruit frangipane tart, 112
  mango mousse with tropical fruit
    salad, 119
  Swiss muesli, 35

g

garlic: baked garlic, 49
  chicken with forty cloves of garlic,
    67
gazpacho, jeweled, 54
ginger: pear, apple, and kiwifruit
    juice with, 126
  Vichy carrots with, 105
glögg, 129
granola, gorgeous, 32
gratin, tomato and eggplant, 92
gravy, rosemary and onion, 75
green shrimp curry, 60
green rice, 102
green Thai curry paste, 136
guacamole with tortilla chips, 14

h

harissa sauce, 136
hazelnuts: dukkah, 17
  hazelnut and raspberry pavlova, 111
horseradish and scallion mash, 102

i

ice cream, raisin rum, 120

j

jam jars, sterilizing, 141
jams: a pot of jam, 141
  uncooked freezer raspberry jam,
    141
jellied bloody marys, 46
jeweled gazpacho, 54

l

lamb: Moroccan butterflied and
    grilled lamb, 25
  pot roast leg of lamb, 75
leek and potato soup, 55
lemon: lemon curd, 141
  lemon curd tartlets, 115
  pussyfoot, 128
  real old-fashioned lemonade, 126
  tagliolini with lemon and green
    olives, 87

white wine sangria, 131
lemongrass: basil and lemongrass
    pesto, 135
  lemongrass syrup, 119
lettuce: Caesar salad, 97
  petits pois à la française, 105
livers: chicken liver parfait, 53

m

mango mousse, 119
maple syrup: mixed nut molasses
    tart, 115
meringues: brown sugar meringues,
    120
  hazelnut and raspberry pavlova, 111
Mexican pork and beans, 29
mint tea, Moroccan, 132
molasses tart, mixed nut, 115
Moroccan butterflied and grilled
    lamb, 25
Moroccan mint tea, 132
moules marinière feast, 63
mousse, mango, 119
muesli, Swiss, 35
muffin mania, 40
mushrooms: mushroom, walnut, and
    goat cheese tart, 83
  steak and wild mushroom pies, 72
mussels: a fabulous paella, 21
  moules marinière feast, 63

n

noodles: cold noodles with peanut
    sauce, 98
  green shrimp curry with thin
    noodles, 60
nuts: dukkah, 17
  gorgeous granola, 32
  mixed nut molasses tart, 115
  nut butter on toast, 39
  oven-roasted spiced nuts, 17

o

oats: gorgeous granola, 32
  oatmeal sodabread, 138
  overnight porridge, 32
  Swiss muesli, 35
olive oil and Parmesan mash, 68
olives: black olive tapenade, 137
  chicken with Tuscan herbs, 68
  tagliolini with lemon and green
    olives, 87
  tapenade toast, 46
onions: bitter orange and onion
    chutney, 53
  caramelized onion confit, 137

felafel with avocado, tomato, and red onion salsa, 84
pissaladière, 88
pot roast leg of lamb with rosemary and onion gravy, 75
simple onion confit, 137
orange: bitter orange and onion chutney, 53
pussyfoot, 128
white wine sangria, 131

p
paella, 21
palmiers, Parmesan, 13
pancetta: a big pot of cassoulet, 26
chicken with Tuscan herbs, 68
perfect roast fillet of beef, 71
sausage and bacon rolls, 39
panna cotta, coffee, 116
Parmesan and rosemary palmiers, 13
pasta: ricotta, basil, and cherry tomato cannelloni, 80
tagliolini with lemon and green olives, 87
pastry: rich short-crust, 112
short-crust, 83
sweet short-crust, 112
pâté: chicken liver parfait, 53
pavlova, hazelnut and raspberry, 111
pear, apple, and kiwi fruit juice, 126
peas: a fabulous paella, 21
petits pois à la française, 105
pesto: basil and lemongrass, 135
salmon steaks with hot pesto and tomatoes, 64
tomato and eggplant gratin with, 92
tomato and chile, 135
walnut and arugula, 135
pies, steak and wild mushroom, 72
pissaladière, 88
pork: Mexican pork and beans, 29
roast loin of pork with balsamic vinegar, 76
porridge, overnight, 32
pot roast leg of lamb, 75
potatoes: leek and potato soup, 55
olive oil and Parmesan mash, 68
perfect mashed potatoes, 102
potatoes dauphinoise, 101
scallion and horseradish mash, 102

prunes in Armagnac or brandy, 139
pussyfoot, 128

r
raspberries: hazelnut and raspberry pavlova, 111
uncooked freezer raspberry jam, 141
ratatouille, 101
red Thai curry paste, 136
rice: a fabulous paella, 21
green rice, 102
smoked salmon and cucumber sushi rolls, 45
ricotta, basil, and cherry tomato cannelloni, 80
rosemary: grilled goat cheese and rosemary bruschetta, 49
Parmesan and rosemary palmiers, 13
pot roast leg of lamb with rosemary and onion gravy, 75
rum: raisin rum ice cream, 120

s
salads: Caesar salad, 97
cucumber salad, 18
fillet of beef salad with Thai dressing, 22
salmon: salmon steaks with hot pesto and tomatoes, 64
whole poached salmon, 18
salsa, avocado, tomato, and red onion, 84
sangria, white wine, 131
sausages: a big pot of cassoulet, 26
sausage and bacon rolls, 39
short-crust pastry, 83, 112
shrimp: a fabulous paella, 21
green shrimp curry, 60
smoked salmon and cucumber sushi rolls, 45
sodabread, oatmeal, 138
soups: chickpea chermoula soup, 56
fiery red bell pepper soup, 56
jeweled gazpacho, 54
leek and potato soup, 55
steak and wild mushroom pies, 72
sterilizing jam jars, 141
strawberries: a pot of jam, 141
sushi rolls, smoked salmon and cucumber, 45
sweet and sour pickled cucumber, 18
Swiss muesli, 35

syrup, lemongrass, 119
Szechuan peppercorns, 98

t
tagliolini with lemon and green olives, 87
tapenade: black olive, 137
tapenade toast, 46
tarts: fruit frangipane tart, 112
lemon curd tartlets, 115
mixed nut molasses tart, 115
mushroom, walnut, and goat cheese tart, 83
pissaladière, 88
tea: Moroccan mint tea, 132
spiced tea, 132
tea-infused fruit compote, 35
Thai curry pastes, 136
Thai dressing, 22
tomato juice: jellied bloody marys, 46
tomatoes: chickpea chermoula soup, 56
felafel with avocado, tomato, and red onion salsa, 84
fiery red bell pepper soup, 56
jeweled gazpacho, 54
Mexican pork and beans, 29
pissaladière, 88
ricotta, basil, and cherry tomato cannelloni, 80
salmon steaks with hot pesto and tomatoes, 64
sesame and mint couscous with winter vegetables, 91
tomato and eggplant gratin, 92
tomato and chile pesto, 135
tortilla chips, guacamole with, 14
truffles, chocolate chile, 123

v
vegetables: ratatouille, 101
roasted Mediterranean vegetables, 106
sesame and mint couscous with winter vegetables, 91
see also individual types of vegetable
Vichy carrots 105

w
walnuts: caramelizing, 116
mushroom, walnut, and goat cheese tart, 83
walnut and arugula pesto, 135
watercress purée, leek and potato soup with, 55

y
Yorkshire puddings, herbed, 71

conversion charts

Weights and measures have been rounded up or down slightly to make measuring easier.

Volume equivalents:

American	Metric	Imperial
1 teaspoon	5 ml	
1 tablespoon	15 ml	
¼ cup	60 ml	2 fl.oz.
⅓ cup	75 ml	2½ fl.oz.
½ cup	125 ml	4 fl.oz.
⅔ cup	150 ml	5 fl.oz. (¼ pint)
¾ cup	175 ml	6 fl.oz.
1 cup	250 ml	8 fl.oz.

Weight equivalents:

Imperial	Metric
1 oz.	25 g
2 oz.	50 g
3 oz.	75 g
4 oz.	125 g
5 oz.	150 g
6 oz.	175 g
7 oz.	200 g
8 oz. (½ lb.)	250 g
9 oz.	275 g
10 oz.	300 g
11 oz.	325 g
12 oz.	375 g
13 oz.	400 g
14 oz.	425 g
15 oz.	475 g
16 oz. (1 lb.)	500 g
2 lb.	1 kg

Measurements:

Inches	Cm
¼ inch	5 mm
½ inch	1 cm
¾ inch	1.5 cm
1 inch	2.5 cm
2 inches	5 cm
3 inches	7 cm
4 inches	10 cm
5 inches	12 cm
6 inches	15 cm
7 inches	18 cm
8 inches	20 cm
9 inches	23 cm
10 inches	25 cm
11 inches	28 cm
12 inches	30 cm

Oven temperatures:

110°C	(225°F)	Gas ¼
120°C	(250°F)	Gas ½
140°C	(275°F)	Gas 1
150°C	(300°F)	Gas 2
160°C	(325°F)	Gas 3
180°C	(350°F)	Gas 4
190°C	(375°F)	Gas 5
200°C	(400°F)	Gas 6
220°C	(425°F)	Gas 7
230°C	(450°F)	Gas 8
240°C	(475°F)	Gas 9